THE
Product
Manager's
Handbook

THE COMPLETE PRODUCT MANAGEMENT RESOURCE

SECOND EDITION

Linda Gorchels

NTC Business Books
NTC/Contemporary Publishing Group

Library of Congress Cataloging-in-Publication Data

Gorchels, Linda.
    The product manager's handbook : the complete product management resource /
Gorchels.—2nd ed.
        p.   cm.
    Includes bibliographical references and index.
    ISBN 0-658-00135-3
    1. Product management.   2. New products—Marketing.   I. Title
HF5415.15.G636   2000
658.8—dc21
                                                                                99-057181

Cover design by Nick Panos
Interior design by Rattray Design

Published by NTC Business Books
A division of NTC/Contemporary Publishing Group, Inc.
4255 West Touhy Avenue, Lincolnwood (Chicago), Illinois 60712-1975 U.S.A.
Copyright © 2000 by Linda Gorchels
Printed in the United States of America
International Standard Book Number: 0-658-00135-3
        04   05   LB   15   14   13   12   11   10   9   8   7   6

CONTENTS

PREFACE

Back to the Future

The changes I have observed in business have been dramatic since the first edition of my book was published. The Internet was a fledgling concept at that time and now it has become a fairly standard part of business. Although globalization was a growing phenomenon prior to my first edition, it has also escalated in importance.

On the other hand, there have been some constants. Through all the turbulence, there remains a need for entrepreneurial spirit, for an ability to work with and through other people, and for a clear and focused direction. These are the characteristics of a product manager acting as the general manager of a "virtual company."

Product management has long been viewed as one of the more effective organizational forms for multiproduct firms. The advantages are numerous and frequently documented. First, it provides a dedicated champion for a product, brand, or service. Second, a healthy internal competitive environment can be created. Third, by championing a number of offerings, a firm can more quickly respond to shifting customer loyalties. And, finally, an opportunity is provided to readily assess candidates for promotion to higher management levels.

Nevertheless, the effectiveness of product management is contingent upon several factors. If we expect product managers to truly champion brands, they must be engaged in both day-to-day decision issues and in developing the strategic future paths of their offerings. Although some companies have created a hierarchical product management structure to do this, effective product management in the future will result from a horizontal decision-making process. Product managers will play a major role in most product-related decisions, while relying on specialists to carry out many of those decisions. The emphasis will be on matching customer needs with corporate capabilities through the development of specific products and services.

Now, to introduce the second edition, I'd like to use the contemporary format (often used in website design) of frequently asked questions (FAQs).

Frequently Asked Questions (FAQs)

What is a product manager?

A product manager is typically a middle manager charged with managing and marketing existing products (and developing new products) for a given product line, brand, or service. Other job titles could include brand manager, industry manager, or customer segment manager. (Note that the term *product* will refer to both products and services.)

What types of companies use product managers?

Product managers are used in all types of companies from consumer packaged goods to services (such as financial institutions) to industrial companies (such as original equipment manufacturers (OEMs), component suppliers, and after-market firms) to nonprofit organizations (such as hospitals).

What's the difference between product management and product development?

Product management is the holistic job of product managers, including planning, forecasting, and marketing products or services. Product development is a corporate process of designing and commercializing new products. This book focuses on product management.

Who should read this book?

This book is targeted most directly at existing product managers and customer segment managers (primarily in "nontraditional" roles beyond consumer packaged goods). However, it has been used effectively by people in all types of companies and industries. Many new product managers and directors or vice presidents of product management or marketing have found it valuable as well.

What will I learn by reading this book?

You'll learn about different approaches to product management from different types of organizations, as well as ideas for getting work done through other functional areas. You'll learn how to develop annual marketing plans for your products and services, with a special emphasis on enhancing customer loyalty and profitability. You'll learn how to strategically evaluate your product portfolio, walk through a typical corporate development process, and prepare for effective launch strategies. And finally, you'll learn various ways to add perceived value both to your product and to your effectiveness as a product manger.

How will I learn these skills?

Several techniques have been used to help you in the learning process: (1) real-world cases showing product management in action, (2) hands-on worksheets for the planning process, and (3) checklists at the end of each chapter for evaluating progress at every critical stage. In addition, this edition has new chapters on the impact of technology on product managers (Chapter 4), customer value management (Chapter 6), and the financial side of product management (Chapter 11).

What feedback did you receive on the first edition?

A review published in the July 1997 issue of the *Journal of Product Innovation Management* stated

> This book is a handy broad-based reference guide describing all aspects of the product management function and relating them to the contemporary and turbulent business climate. . . . It provides a realistic overview of the many roles product managers play and it examines, in an organized fashion, a variety of management tools which may be employed to maximize the value of the product manager.

The book is valuable because it provides theoretic frameworks [for] identifying, analyzing, and managing product lines while supporting those approaches with relevant and recognizable case studies to clearly illustrate the points being made.[1]

A customer review from Amazon.com stated:

Product Management is one of those jobs that is different for each product manager; what it is depends on your product and what you make of it. The danger is that when you write about product management, you focus on your specific experience. I found this book to be general enough to be of interest to many; still it was not so high-level that it did not provide any help. I would recommend this book to everyone who thinks about product management as a next career. I would also recommend it to those who have been in product management for several years, and just want to read what others think about it.

In addition, since the book has been used as part of an executive education program sponsored by the School of Business at the University of Wisconsin–Madison, it has been reviewed by hundreds of product managers and has received high marks for practicality and usefulness.

Is the book available internationally?

Yes, the book has had increasing international sales and the first edition was translated into Spanish.

ACKNOWLEDGMENTS

My interest in product management began several years ago when I realized that the term meant significantly different things to different companies. Several people contributed to this growing awareness, including participants at my product management workshops, sponsored by the Executive Education department of the School of Business at the University of Wisconsin–Madison. I found numerous examples of nontraditional approaches to the subject, and widely varying success factors. This book highlights some of those findings. In addition, several product managers responded to E-mail inquiries about their positions and supplied example job descriptions. I want to thank all those individuals for their willingness to provide input for the revision of the book.

Part I

The Role and Operation of Product Management

The ability to attract and retain high-profit customers is a distinguishing characteristic of successful businesses, and many companies struggle with how to attain that goal. To succeed, firms employ many different strategies, including competency management; customer retention programs; strategic leveraging; global marketing; project management; big, hairy, audacious goals (BHAGs); E-commerce; and supply chain management. Yet all of the tools and techniques espoused by management gurus have not replaced the importance of a solid organizational structure to guide an organization in accomplishing corporate goals. One such organizational structure that has withstood the test of time in many situations is the product management structure. In this type of structure, product managers oversee a set of defined products or services that face different competitors and different customer constraints than many or all of the other products and services in the company. Determining if product management is the optimal structure for a particular company involves a number of considerations, including the company's culture; how much technical knowledge is required to design, launch, and support specific products; and whether the company's products require distinctly different approaches to "going to market."

Once a structure is established, clarifying the roles of company personnel with whom product managers routinely interact is important. The product manager is a generalist who must rely on numerous functional specialists to develop and market the product line. The product manager is the liaison among the functional departments within the company as well as among the company, the sales force, and the customers for all product-related issues. As a result, some understanding of mutual expectations is appropriate.

On an ongoing basis, product managers exchange information with the sales force. They represent the voice of the customer at internal meetings on the product line in question. And they need to plan for current and future product activities that benefit the company as a whole.

Part I discusses the evolution of product management, provides suggestions for selecting the "right" product managers and managing the system effectively, and demonstrates the need for product managers to be cross-functional leaders.

1

The New Product Management

THERE HAS BEEN an evolution in product management over the past decade. Rather than declining in number and importance as had been forecast in numerous articles, product management (especially "non-traditional" product, market, and service management) has prevailed by encompassing customer management and value chain analysis, evolving into a more holistic position. The overall responsibility of a product manager is to integrate the various segments of a business into a strategically focused whole, maximizing the value of a product by coordinating the "production" of an offering with an understanding of market needs. To accomplish this, a product manager needs a broad knowledge of virtually all aspects of a company along with very focused knowledge of a specific product or product line and its customers. Product managers manage not only products, but projects and processes as well.

Procter & Gamble has been credited with the creation of the product management concept. In 1931, Camay soap was languishing while Ivory soap was thriving. A Procter & Gamble executive suggested that an individual manager be assigned responsibility for Camay, in effect pitting the brands against each other. This brand-management system was so successful that it was copied by most consumer packaged goods companies.[1]

Product management is a matrix organizational structure in which a product manager is charged with the success of a product or product line but has no direct authority over the individuals producing and selling the product. Much of the work of a product manager is through various departments and cross-functional teams, almost as if the product manager were operating a business within a business. (See feature The Life of a Consumer-Brand Product Manager.)

There are both advantages and disadvantages to the product management approach. On the plus side, a product manager provides dedicated attention to a product line. This results in better information about the customers, competition, and strategic potential for that group of products. In addition, since the product manager must necessarily interact with the various operational units of a company, the position can provide a good training ground for young executives. On the other hand, one common criticism of the product management structure is that it is a "fast-track" or "stepping-stone" position, overemphasizing short-term results. It also promotes the perception that product management skills are more transferable than product and industry knowledge. In addition, product management can cause conflict because the product manager has limited functional authority over many parts of the development, marketing, and sales of the product, but may nevertheless have bottom-line responsibility. Finally, product managers might focus on the product almost to the exclusion of the customer.

Despite its limitations, product management (or some variation of it) has found its way into virtually every type of industry, going well beyond the traditional consumer-product brand-manager position. Even within fast-moving consumer packaged goods companies, product management has evolved. However, because of the increasing level of internal brand cannibalization and competition for resources, along with media fragmentation and a higher level of retail and consumer sophistication, product management is being stretched into different "shapes."

Product Management Today

Product management as an organizational form has moved into a variety of business-to-business firms, as well as service organizations such as financial institutions and hospitals. Most large banks have product managers for credit cards, deposit services, trust operations, and com-

The Life of a Consumer-Brand Product Manager

Tracy Carlson, senior product manager for Lever Brothers' Wisk detergent, spends an inordinate amount of time with stains. In an effort to move her brand to become the best-selling liquid laundry detergent in the country, she has to convince consumers of the superiority of her product over Procter & Gamble's Tide. Like her counterparts at other consumer-product companies, Carlson is responsible for nearly every aspect of her product.

More than being simply champions for their brands, product managers are viewed in some ways as running their own little businesses. They not only oversee product development, but also monitor advertising and promotion, as well as negotiate to obtain shelf space from retailers. With current product proliferation, manufacturers concede that there are few lasting competitive advantages from which to attain market dominance. Therefore, sensitivity, intelligence, and intuition are important traits for product managers facing these battles.

But the real challenge of the job for product managers like Carlson is often simply getting the product onto shelves. A glut of new products has made retailers reluctant to open shelf space without generous inducements from manufacturers. The inducements include paying for in-store displays, fees for mentioning the product in store advertising circulars, and compensation for the increased processing costs of warehousing the new products.

Carlson will not reveal the Wisk marketing budget, but she said that in general the proportion of consumer-products budgets for trade and consumer promotions has risen from less than half to as much as three-fourths, with the balance going to advertising.

Source: Condensed from "High Stakes for Product Managers," *The New York Times* (December 4, 1989): D1–D7.

mercial cash management services.[2] Property/casualty insurers have begun to utilize product managers for highly competitive, rapidly changing lines such as workers' compensation and auto insurance.[3]

Hospitals have also experienced success with the product management structure. A study published in the *Journal of Health Care Marketing* reported that hospitals with product-line management outperformed those without it on virtually all performance indicators, including occupancy rate, gross patient revenue per bed, average profit margin, and return on assets.[4] Not surprisingly, the implementation of product-line management increased with level of competition and hospital bed size. Other health care studies found that product-line management in hospitals offered the benefits of increased accountability, elimination of duplication of services, and a better market orientation. The limitations included a possible increase in costs (because functional management was not eliminated) and an increased need for more timely and accurate data.[5]

Even though traditional product management has had its successes, companies have increasingly modified their approach to product management to incorporate a focus on the customer. This has taken many forms. Some service firms have created what is in fact segment management (even though the product manager title might still be used). For example, hospitals might have a product manager for women's services. Financial institutions might have a small-business product manager or an "affluent market" manager. Deregulation in financial services has contributed to this latter phenomenon. Interest-bearing checking accounts, money market funds, affinity credit cards, and an explosion of other product offerings attempt to appeal to increasingly smaller market segments. This, along with the availability of more sophisticated technology, has changed the focus of product management at banks.

> [In one year alone], banks launched about 700 new affinity programs, and customers opened 7.5 million new affinity accounts. The aim of product proliferation has been to satisfy an increasingly divergent set of customer needs. To keep track of these divergent needs, banks have invested in customer information file (CIF) technologies that permit segmentation across many dimensions, only one of which is product. The data generated by CIFs have accelerated the growth of market-segment-focused strategies.[6]

Segment management has been successful at several banks. (See feature Segment Management in Financial Services.) Simply shifting the emphasis from products to segments, however, will not eliminate some of the problems that can exist in a matrix organization. A matrix organization is one in which people report directly to a specific function area, but report indirectly (through a "dotted-line" relationship) to other functional areas. Both—or neither—can result in an enhanced understanding of customers and an ability to satisfy their needs. It requires a commitment to make it work.

First, there must be a clear understanding of the basic rationale for product management as an organizational form. Product management is generally most successful for companies with several products having similar manufacturing but different marketing requirements, particularly when the same product cuts across several divisions or customer groups. Second, top management must be committed to the product management organization and provide the structure and tools to make it work. And, finally, the right people must be selected and developed for the job.

Product Management Tomorrow

Product management will continue to evolve to meet the needs of the market and of the particular company employing it. Consumer goods product managers, for example, will find it necessary to be more involved with the trade as retailers gain more knowledge of and "influence" with consumers. Consequently, they will need to think more in terms of category management. Category management involves looking at a line (i.e., category) of products as it might be evaluated by a market segment (i.e., retailer). To accomplish this, product managers might need to work together as a category team. Or a category manager position might be established to oversee all products and product managers related to a given market segment.

Another trend that might affect the future role of product managers is the use of product management teams. As companies continue to escalate their involvement with team-based decisions, product management teams (PMTs) will appear in some companies. Global companies will have cross-border product business teams responsible for leveraging capabilities throughout the world. These will be "virtual teams," which do not meet regularly on a face-to-face basis and are not located in the same country. Although project teams have been very successful in new-product development, the appropriateness of *ongoing*

Segment Management in Financial Services

Banks that have traditionally used product managers have generally assigned them to groups of deposit products, home equity loans, mortgages, insurance, and so on. Unfortunately, these products are not always complementary, and they might even be considered indirect substitutes by consumers. Therefore, banks such as Sovran Financial and Bank One/Texas have experimented with segment management.

Sovran Financial Corp., a holding company for four Middle Atlantic banks, reorganized its marketing structure to replace product management with a market segment emphasis. Sovran had attempted a relationship marketing strategy before the structure change, but found it difficult to implement with an organization by product. Therefore, in 1988, it reorganized by individual market segments, such as the "affluent market." The segment management design allowed Sovran to capture what it referred to as "share of wallet," which increased from 38 percent to 46 percent in Virginia and from 44 percent to 62 percent in Tennessee.

At Bank One/Texas, one of the product managers is the small business market segment manager, responsible for developing marketing programs to support the branches and sales force in bringing in new small businesses to the bank. This position has enabled Bank One to package products appropriate for a specific segment's needs.

Source: Condensed from Eric Berggren and Robert Dewar, "Is Product Management Obsolete?" *Journal of Retail Banking* 13 (Winter 1991/1992): 30; Lauryn Franzoni, "Product Managers: Finding the Right Fit," *Bank Marketing* 23 (May 1991): 28+.

teams in charge of existing products will have to be carefully considered and structured before implementation.

Regardless of the organizational changes product management may undergo in the future, successful product managers must thoroughly understand the needs of various segments within the market, appreciate the corporate competencies available in the company, and be able to leverage these competencies to meet market needs. In other words, the ultimate goal of the product manager will be customer satisfaction obtained by being a cross-functional leader in the firm.

The Product Manager's Job

The product manager's job is to oversee all aspects of a product/service line to create and deliver superior customer satisfaction while simultaneously providing long-term value for the company. To accomplish this, there will be various day-to-day, short-term, and long-term activities. Ideally, day-to-day activities provide the foundation for the job of the product manager and usually absorb 40–55 percent of a product manager's time; 20–30 percent of the time is devoted to short-term activities; and 15–25 percent is allotted to long-term tasks. (This, of course, varies depending on the time of the fiscal year, the relative proportion of new versus mature products managed, as well as a host of other variables.) These percentages are goals. Unfortunately, the reality is that many product managers spend too much time "putting out fires," to the exclusion of strategic planning. (See Figure 1.1.) Time management is crucial for all businesspeople, and product managers are no exception.

A recent national survey of product managers showed that a significant proportion of product managers spent much time responding to sales force requests and expediting products through other departments but wished they could spend less time on those activities. This same survey found that product managers spent little time developing long-range strategy for products and contacting customers to understand future needs/applications but wished they could spend more time in these ways.[7]

Day-to-Day Duties

On a day-to-day basis, the product manager might have the following responsibilities:

- Maintain a product fact book.
- Motivate the sales force and distributors.
- Collect marketing information, including competitive benchmarks, trends and opportunities, and customer expectations.

Figure 1.1 The Product Manager's Balance of Activities

- Act as a liaison between sales, manufacturing, research and development (R & D), and so on.
- Control the budget and achieve sales goals.

Short-Term Duties

On a short-term (e.g., fiscal year) basis, the product manager might have the following responsibilities:

- Participate in annual marketing-plan and forecast development.
- Work with advertising departments/agencies to implement promotional strategies.
- Coordinate trade shows/conventions.
- Initiate regulatory acceptance.
- Participate in new-product development teams.
- Predict and manage competitors' actions.
- Modify product and/or reduce costs to increase value.
- Recommend line extensions.
- Participate in product-elimination decisions.

Long-Term Duties

On a long-term (strategic) basis, the product manager might have the following responsibilities:

- Create a long-term competitive strategy for the product.
- Identify new-product opportunities.
- Recommend product changes, enhancements, and introductions.

Historically, the product manager's job has varied somewhat between consumer and business-to-business firms. Consumer product managers typically managed fewer products and spent more time on advertising and sales promotion. The target markets were generally larger (millions rather than thousands or hundreds), with a greater potential for diversity. Business product managers tended to be more involved in the technical aspects of the product or service and spent more time with engineering and the sales force.

However, the gap between the two types of product managers is narrowing. Fragmentation of consumer markets has escalated, resulting in greater product proliferation and parity products, for which consumers perceive little distinction in features or quality and usually make purchase decisions based on price. Trade satisfaction is becoming more critical as mass merchandisers and other "category killers" such as Wal-Mart, Home Depot, and Office Max are gaining momentum. As a result, consumer product managers are finding themselves more involved with salespeople and the trade (e.g., retailers). On the business-to-business side, product managers are finding a growing need to introduce advertising to their firms and to establish a more solid position against an ever-increasing number of competitors. Market (as opposed to product) knowledge has become a key determinant of successful differentiation.

The Global Product Manager

A global product manager is not simply one who oversees products sold in other countries. The global product manager is one who thinks and plans with an appreciation of the global competitive arena. Even companies with a low percentage of foreign sales have global competitors, global suppliers, and global customers. Global *thinking* is important for these product managers, not just sales. Whether or not a company has multinational locations, global product managers develop long-term product strategies on a global basis. They look for similarities across different world markets, standardizing whenever possible and customizing whenever necessary. This affords opportunities (proactively) for future foreign sales as well as for competitive strategies against global competitors.

Global strategy for product managers means embedding both domestic and international standards into products and services at the point of design, not as afterthoughts. This implies meeting world standards even before seeking foreign markets, while simultaneously acknowledging national differences and local norms. This approach has the obvious advantage of taking into consideration the needs of major markets right at the start, rather than having to retrofit a product developed for one national market.

Product managers start by identifying globally strategic markets and then analyzing the needs of those markets. By searching for commonalities (as well as differences) product managers necessarily think in terms of platform design for global products. Product managers are wise to design the largest possible standardized core, while allowing for necessary customization at the same time. The main goal of the product-development process is not to develop a standard product or product line but to build adaptability into products and product lines to achieve worldwide appeal.

The idea of a fully standardized global product that is identical all over the world is a near myth. Some of the benefits of global products (or services), however, can be achieved by standardizing the core product or large parts of it, while customizing peripheral or other parts of the product. In passenger automobiles, for example, product standardization comes primarily in the "platform" (the chassis and related parts) and to a lesser extent the engine. The auto industry has been talking about global cars for decades, but implementation has been difficult at best. Honda made progress with its 1998 Accord. By coming up with a platform that can be bent and stretched into markedly different vehicles, Honda saved hundreds of millions of dollars in development costs. By moving the car's gas tank back between the rear tires, Honda engineers discovered they could design a series of special brackets that would allow them to hook the wheels to the car's more flexible inner subframe. Rather than shipping the same car around the globe, only the underlying platform will be used worldwide.

Regardless of the attempt to standardize products or product lines globally, various levels of adaptation are required. Some products need only different language documentation. For example, when Minolta cameras are shipped from Japan to New Wave Enterprise, a distribution center at the Port of Antwerp in Belgium, they are shipped without support materials. Language-specific documentation (e.g., French, Dutch, German) is added when the products are shipped across land to other destinations in Europe.

Other products could have their life cycles extended by looking for the best fit between market needs and product capabilities. For example, the current U.S. technology for anesthesia ventilators allows plus or minus a few milliliters of oxygen accuracy. However, many Latin American operating rooms are satisfied with plus or minus 100 milliliters of accuracy, with a commensurately lower price. A major supplier of anesthesia equipment found it could prolong the life of its "unsophisticated" ventilators by offering them in these markets at a much lower price than the "state-of-the-art" equipment.

This approach can apply to consumer products as well. Take basic flour as an example. India consumes about 69 million tons of wheat a year (compared to 26 million tons in the United States), yet almost no whole-wheat flour is sold prepackaged. Selling packaged flour in India is almost revolutionary, since most Indian housewives still buy raw wheat in bulk, clean it by hand, and on a weekly basis carry some to a neighborhood mill, or *chakki*, where it is ground between two stones. Pillsbury found it could increase the sales of basic prepackaged flour (a mature product in the United States) by appealing to this market and has modified the Pillsbury Doughboy to pitch this "old" product as something new in India.

With increasing competition able to react quickly when new products are introduced, worldwide planning at the product level provides a number of tangible benefits. First, product managers are better able to develop products with specifications compatible on a global scale. Second, they are able to more effectively and efficiently adapt products to local needs. And third, they are able to respond more quickly to competitive moves of global companies.

Checklist: The New Product Manager

✓ To ensure that you focus on the long-term value of a product, do not view your product manager role as a "fast-track" or "stepping-stone" position.

✓ Be careful not to lose sight of the customer as you strive to create competitively superior products and services.

✓ If you have specific groups of customers who require unique products, or if you must combine standard products in unique ways to meet the needs of these customer groups, consider segment management as an alternative (or in addition) to product management.

✓ Expect the role of product manager to continue to evolve to meet current business challenges. Category management and the use of product management teams will be tested by companies striving to improve competitive performance.

✓ Balance your activities among day-to-day, short-term, and long-term activities to avoid the trap of constantly "putting out fires."

✓ As your company begins multinational moves, your job should start with global thinking rather than global sales:

- Embed both domestic and international standards into products and services.
- Look for common needs among globally strategic markets and standardize the core product.
- Identify the appropriate level of country adaptation required for your product.
- Anticipate global competition.

2

Introducing Product Management and Managing Product Managers

SHIFTING FROM A functional (silo) organizational structure to any of a variety of team or matrix-based organizational forms (including product management) requires careful planning. Job descriptions must be written to help the product managers understand their new roles, and other departments must understand what to expect from the new positions. Product managers must rely on the support and performance of many others in the organization to achieve product performance goals, even though they have no control over those functions. Clarification of objectives is imperative for the successful introduction of a product management structure in an organization. Unfortunately, many companies introduce the title "product manager" because their competitors have such a position, but they lack understanding of what the position entails.

There are four steps involved in initiating product management. First, the company must assess whether product management is the appropriate organizational form and, if it is appropriate, decide what reporting structure (hierarchy) it will have. Second, the company must clearly specify the responsibilities of product managers as well as other integral members of the system. Third, characteristics of successful product managers must be identified, with suitable personnel recruited

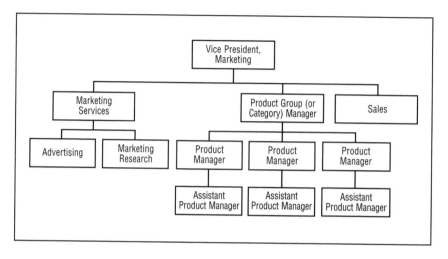

Figure 2.1 Traditional Product Management Organization

for the product management openings. And, fourth, there must be a system for developing and evaluating product managers. Each of these steps is discussed in detail in this chapter.

Assessing the Need for and Structure of Product Management

Product management can be an appropriate organizational structure when a company's product line has grown to the point where a functional structure no longer works. There might be more products than a single marketing manager can handle, even though these could flow into a common market through the same channels. Or the company's products might be so different from each other in terms of competition and customer groups that they must be handled differently. Or technical or sophisticated product knowledge might be required to meet the needs of the market. In this case, the product manager might be involved in the development and marketing of a product line across various divisions or markets. (See Figure 2.1.)

On the other hand, there are subtle variations that might be appropriate under different circumstances. (See Figure 2.2.) If the industry's products are primarily "parity" (essentially the same) in the minds of

Product/Market Characteristics	Possible Organizational Structure
Many products going to a limited number of market segments. The products require focused attention to be fully successful.	Product management
Company sells to a variety of market segments with preferences for various product sets. The products might not require elaborate customization, but the "bundling" of products is unique to the market segments.	Market or segment management
The same situation as above, but there is also a need to develop some new products for various market segments.	Segment management with "special products" managers
The company sells to a few large customers with differing needs from the rest of the customer base.	Key account management
New-product efforts are time-consuming and critical for the company, to the point where a special position is created exclusively to handle new products.	Product development manager or new-products manager, possibly (although not necessarily) part of a technical department

Figure 2.2 Appropriate Organizational Structures for Various Product/Market Types

the customers, a traditional product manager structure might result in pressure to create artificial differences simply for the sake of differentiation. In this case, a market or segment management approach might be preferred. Market managers are used when a company needs to develop different markets for a single product line. Focus is on developing the market rather than on taking the product to market. The market manager would "bundle" and/or adapt combinations of a company's products to fit the needs of select market segments. There might or might not also be a need to have "special products" managers in conjunction with segment managers.

A variation of market management is key account or national account management. With the emergence of "category killers" and other large customers, key account managers have been given the responsibility of working with major accounts to determine how products can best be adapted to meet their needs. If product managers are spending an inordinate amount of time handling special requests for major customers, a key account position could focus on the "special requests" and work with the product manager on product adaptation.

The Impact of New-Product Development

The last major consideration in organizational structure is related to new-product development. Although most product managers spend a significant part of their time on new-product development activities, some companies choose to have a separate new-product manager position to handle the specifications and design of products, with the product managers following through with the marketing activities. Although this is less common (and perhaps less desirable if customer input is an afterthought), it is an organizational form that can fit certain needs.

Implementing a Global Structure

As mentioned in Chapter 1, product managers should generally be familiar with the global environment for their products if they deal with global suppliers, customers with global locations, or competitors with foreign operations. For global companies, there's an additional level of complexity. Companies must decide whether a single product manager has global authority for a product, whether product managers should interact with country managers, or whether there should be country-specific product managers. At minimum, the product manager will be involved in cross-cultural teams charged with leveraging the skills of different parts of a global company located in different parts of the world. As Whirlpool CEO David Whitwam said in an interview with *Harvard Business Review*,

The only way to gain lasting competitive advantage is to leverage your capabilities around the world so that the company as a whole is greater than the sum of its parts. Being an international company—selling globally, having global brands or operations in different countries—isn't enough.

Let me use washing machines as an example. Washing technology is washing technology. But our German products are feature-rich and thus considered to be higher-end. The products that come out of our Italian plants run at lower RPMs and are less costly. Still, the reality is that the insides of the machines don't vary a great deal. Both the German and the Italian washing machines can be standardized and simplified by reducing the number of parts, which is true of any product family. Yet when we bought Philips, the washing machines made in the Italian and German facilities didn't have one screw in common. Today products are being designed to ensure that a wide variety of models can be built on the same basic platform. Our new dryer line has precisely this kind of common platform, and other product categories are currently being designed in the same way.[1]

Reducing Hierarchy

Most product managers are part of a marketing or marketing/sales department, usually reporting to a marketing or product management director, a marketing or product management manager, or a vice president of marketing. Product managers frequently have no one reporting to them. In larger firms, however, product managers might have assistants and associates reporting to them, as well as authority over some functional subordinates. Some product managers have eight or more people reporting to them directly. If there are to be staff under the product manager, it's usually best to provide information processors, coordinators, or analysts, rather than proliferating pyramids of assistants and associates, creating a hierarchy within a hierarchy.

Hierarchies are designed to prevent mistakes, but they also diminish individual responsibility, creativity, and risk-taking opportunities. That's why so many management gurus have espoused variations of the horizontal corporation, with an emphasis on providing better products and services for the end customer. Product managers and product management teams are consistent with this philosophy if they are linked to customer satisfaction (as they should be) and given the authority to make relevant decisions regarding their product lines.

Specifying Responsibilities of Product Managers and Others in the Firm

To minimize the potential for miscommunication and misunderstanding and to increase the chances of a successful product management structure, management must thoroughly explain to key managers exactly how the organizational concept will work and what the underlying rationale is for moving to it. It's important to specify not only the roles of product managers, but also the roles of the individuals with whom they commonly interact. Let's take a hypothetical example of a company with three product managers, a marketing services manager, a marketing research manager, and regional sales managers. (All of these people might report to a marketing director or a vice president of marketing/sales.)

Typically, the product managers would recommend and establish strategic guidelines for their products, obtain market information about their customer segments and products, provide input to sales for the closing of selected accounts, and play a major role in product/service development, modifications, and elimination. The marketing services manager would support the product managers by providing communication materials and handling company-wide promotional and public relations activities. The marketing research manager would contract out or conduct marketing research activities required to fully understand customer needs and competitive capabilities and provide input into company growth and acquisition opportunities. The regional sales managers would provide the day-to-day motivation and management of the sales force and support the product managers in the introduction of new products.

Many product managers (particularly in business-to-business companies or in the service sector) are hired for their technical expertise with a specific product or service. Therefore, the roles of the product management function and the related operational functions need to be clarified. For example, the product manager might supply customer and competitor data in support of a recommended new product but leave the actual design to the design staff.

Although these descriptions of responsibilities would not be appropriate for every organization, it's important to think through and define the related responsibilities and overlaps. Providing a summary of role responsibilities before introducing product management will reduce uncertainties about the organizational structure.

Where product managers are positioned in a company can also significantly influence their role, regardless of the responsibilities put in writing. A critical issue for management is to establish a balance between product managers' administrative and entrepreneurial functions. Product managers with a relatively low perceived status cannot become true change agents. On the other hand, product managers with a relatively high-perceived status should have the skills and earned respect required to perform effectively.

A major service-sector firm, introducing product management for the first time, created a task force charged with establishing a model of product manager responsibilities along with the responsibilities of ten support areas (plus senior and business unit management) as they related to product management. The product managers were charged with many of the specific activities listed in this chapter. An abbreviated summary of the responsibilities of the ten support areas is listed in Figure 2.3. Once the structure of product management is installed, management must select the right people and monitor and coach their activities to make sure they stay on track.

Characteristics of Successful Product Managers

There is no ideal profile of a successful product manager. However, several traits, skills, and experiences are frequently identified as related to product management success. Frequently cited traits looked for in product managers include an entrepreneurial attitude, leadership, and self-confidence. Acquired abilities should include organizational, time-management, and communication skills. Sales proficiency and technical competence are also important in many industries. The importance of prior experience depends on the particular needs of the product management position. If highly technical, engineering-oriented knowledge is required, a background in engineering is appropriate. If an understanding of customer applications is desired, a sales background in the industry is appropriate. If knowledge of large-market trends and competitive positioning is important, marketing research and/or advertising experience are desirable.

Senior Vice President

- Setting overall direction and priorities of the organization
- Allocating overall resources

Business Unit Manager

- Approving annual product business plans and budgets
- Determining product resource allocation

Product Development

- Conducting feasibility studies of new products/major enhancements
- Coordinating the development and introduction of new products

Market Research

- Measuring, tracking, and reporting product market shares
- Conducting product research as requested

Marketing and Communications

- Developing and coordinating product-related marketing and sales communication
- Assisting in the development of marketing plans
- Executing marketing plans

Sales

- Prospecting for new business opportunities
- Closing sales

Operations

- Providing routine customer support and service
- Providing product operational efficiency

Corporate Relations

- Identifying new business opportunities and retention strategies
- Coordinating corporate business development plans

Personnel

- Developing and implementing a product manager professional development plan
- Conducting product manager specialized skill training

Quality Assurance

- Assisting in the development and monitoring of quality standards
- Providing process improvement evaluations

Figure 2.3 Responsibilities Established by a Major Financial
Services Company

The appropriate characteristics of a product manager also depend on the culture of the organization and the expectations placed on the position. Some product managers provide (and are expected to provide) a coordinator role; others may be more directive; and still others take on a leadership role.

Product managers who are coordinators primarily function as administrators to assure deadlines are met and requests are carried out. Coordinative product managers are more likely to deal with budgets than plans. Product managers who are directive not only coordinate projects but also develop product plans. Product managers who are leaders are more entrepreneurial and become more active in the strategic planning of products and services for the company.

Part of the difference among desired product manager characteristics depends on whether they work for consumer or industrial product manufacturers. A study of senior marketing executives from Australian companies with a product management organization found differences in management expectations between consumer and industrial firms. Marketing executives from consumer goods firms tended to view product managers as coordinators or implementers of strategy to a greater degree than was true for industrial firms. On the other hand, a greater importance was placed on forecasting and competitor intelligence for industrial product managers than was true for consumer product managers. This is partly because of the wealth of syndicated data available about consumers that is absent in many industrial channels.[2]

This same study highlighted some problems with the product management concept (PMC).

> Those companies who expressed dissatisfaction with the PMC were asked in an open-ended question to explain their reasons. The range of reasons embraced the following: product managers spent too much time on day-to-day matters and not enough on planning and searching for new opportunities; product managers were not sufficiently entrepreneurial; product managers did not have enough authority over the sales department and had poor communication with the sales force (the most frequently mentioned responses); there was poor understanding of product manager role; product managers were inexperienced; and there was an authority-responsibility mismatch.[3]

Developing and Evaluating Product Managers

Product managers need a variety of knowledge, including product/ industry knowledge, business knowledge, and interpersonal/management knowledge. Since beginning product managers typically spend most of their time gathering and organizing information on the product, its customers, and the competition, product knowledge is paramount. As they gain experience, the focus shifts to more comprehensive business knowledge, including finance, marketing, and strategic planning. At the same time, they develop team-building, negotiation, communication, and leadership abilities.

Many companies believe it takes from three to five years to develop an effective product manager. According to Bill Meserve, a principal at the management-consulting firm of Temple, Barker & Sloane Inc., training and motivation are critical at this time, and career development must be an obligation: "The formal approach used at one 3M division is based on a written career development document and scheduled annual reviews, which are separate from performance appraisal. Primary responsibility for monitoring career development rests with senior marketing management or a separate marketing council."[4]

For product managers to be effective, they need to build bridges throughout the company and be cross-functional leaders. Therefore, in the selection and development of product managers, this ability to transcend functional lines must be considered. The downfall of several product or brand management systems was the establishment of a product manager as caretaker of the product, with an emphasis on "safe" results. Product managers were charged with immediate results rather than the creation of long-term customer value. When this happens, product managers focus on improving their own position rather than that of the company's product. According to William Weilbacher in his book *Brand Marketing,*

> In the end, the brand manager is forced by the brand-management system to pay more attention to career management than to brand management. Brand championship and brand advocacy are replaced by actions that make the brand manager look good to management, no matter what the long-term effect upon the brand or the perceptions of the consumers who buy it.[5]

Appropriate evaluation criteria depend on the performance expectations of management. Sales and/or profit goals are fairly common measures of performance. However, if profit is a measure, it's important to distinguish between profit contribution and bottom-line profit. Profit contribution is the amount of product revenue remaining after subtracting all of a product manager's direct, controllable, or relevant expenses. This contribution to overhead (CTO) figure is a fairer assessment of performance than is fully allocated profit, because CTO minimizes the concern over the validity of the allocation methodology. Obsessive attention to allocating overhead against each product often consumes effort that could be better spent elsewhere. This isn't meant to imply that total overhead doesn't need to be covered. The CTO goal is established to cover anticipated overhead allocations but doesn't hold product managers responsible for overhead increases beyond their control.

Some companies implementing quality management principles have opted to minimize individual performance measures and focus on company performance. This does not have to be an either/or decision. Metrics can be designed to measure both individual and corporate performance. Companies can weigh these metrics differently depending on their corporate philosophies on performance measurement.

In addition to financial measures, product managers may be evaluated on some combination of other factors, such as the following:

- Successful introduction of new products
- Market share defense or growth
- Customer satisfaction indexes
- Attainment of company-specific goals

Checklist: Keys to Product Management Success

✓ Recognize product management as an organizational business form, not as an isolated job function.

✓ Prevent product management from being done in the absence of market management. Otherwise, you run the risk of being production-driven rather than market-driven.

✓ Develop an information system of cost, business, and market data according to the relevant products or product lines.

✓ Clarify the roles of product managers and the roles of those with whom they routinely interact.

✓ Push product managers to evolve from being solely product specialists to being cross-functional leaders.

✓ Establish performance goals that reflect company expectations and provide the tools (budgets, people resources, approval authority) to achieve the goals.

✓ Select product managers with the skills appropriate for the culture, expectations, and responsibilities for your company. Provide additional training as required.

3

The Cross-Functional
Role of Product Managers

AFTER THE DECISION is made to introduce product management, or if there is a desire to improve the functioning of an existing structure, the role and activities of product managers must be defined in some detail. A product manager, by definition, is a generalist who must rely on numerous functional specialists to get the product or service to the customer. These specialists can be internal or external to the company. The presence of internal support groups (such as advertising and marketing research) means that product managers can be less technically skilled in these areas and instead focus on managing. However, the product manager's control over the internal groups may be less than over an external group because he or she lacks direct authority. A charge-back system can provide more budget control for the product manager as well as relate costs more effectively to products.

A primary role of product managers is to get all functions to focus on the market—the final customers. Therefore, they must interact directly with various functions in the organization, including sales, operations, finance, customer service, and top management. The extent of interaction will vary by company and the experience level of the product manager. (See feature Product Managers in the Electronics Marketplace.) This chapter discusses some of the typical relationships of a product manager within an organization. Figure 3.1 shows the results of a recent survey that asked product managers to indicate the extent

29

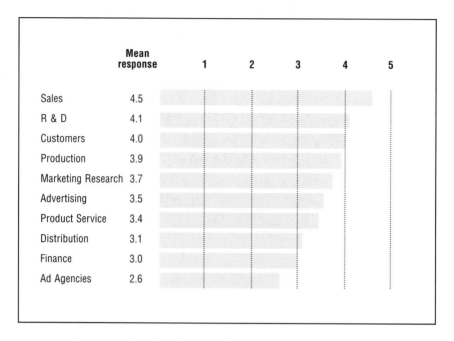

	Mean response	1	2	3	4	5
Sales	4.5					
R & D	4.1					
Customers	4.0					
Production	3.9					
Marketing Research	3.7					
Advertising	3.5					
Product Service	3.4					
Distribution	3.1					
Finance	3.0					
Ad Agencies	2.6					

Figure 3.1 Product Manager Contact with Selected Groups

of contact they have with a variety of areas on a scale from 1 (no contact at all) to 5 (very high level of contact). The groups with which product managers had the greatest level of contact were sales, research and development (R & D), and customers. The mean, or average, responses for each area are shown in the right column of Figure 3.1.

Depending on the company and situation, the product manager plays various roles in terms of support activities. With regard to field sales, the product manager answers questions from the field, assists on sales calls as needed, provides product information to simplify the sales process, suggests various incentives for new products, and/or develops literature and other customer pieces to help further the sales effort. With regard to distribution, the product manager might work with distributors or agents, suggest alternative channels, and/or expedite shipments. Figure 3.2 shows some of the groups with which product managers frequently interact. Those in bold circles generally have the highest interaction. However, all of these functions may turn to the product manager as the "answer person," requiring the product manager to be diplomatic in time management.

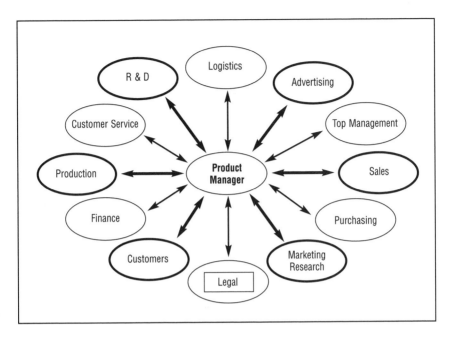

Figure 3.2 Product Management: Primary Role Influencers

Sales

The product manager plays a major role in helping salespeople accomplish the objectives of the company (not to mention the objectives of the salespeople themselves). The nature of the relationship varies according to the culture of the organization and the positioning of product management. A coordinative product manager is likely to be heavily committed to sales support and "putting out fires." The position won't generate a desire on the part of sales to provide market intelligence or push the product. At the other extreme, an authoritarian product manager who expects to provide minimal support to the sales force will get minimal support back from them as well. This type of product manager might attempt to use home-office authority to "force" sales cooperation and can severely damage the trust and respect required for a cooperative effort.

Gathering Market Data from the Sales Force

Salespeople provide a critical link to the customer, and effective product managers appreciate the need for this knowledge. Consequently,

Product Managers in the Electronics Marketplace

The electronics field is known for short product life cycles and fragmented customer segments. Competition and price pressure are intense. Facing these challenges, the product manager must be able to work with and through a variety of individuals.

The product manager's position will, of course, vary by company, as Bill Meserve points out in his *Electronic Business* article, "The Changing Role of Product Management":

> At one components division of General Instrument Corp., product managers function mostly as coordinators between engineering product development and marketing, and between marketing and sales. They have direct responsibility for product line advertising and promotion budgets, but only provide marketing input to product development projects, which are initiated and managed by engineering. Hewlett-Packard Co. product managers, in contrast, are frequently the focal point for new product development. They prepare the product development plan, authorize its implementation and monitor its progress.

Regardless of the role given a product manager by a company, the product manager must develop management skills to be able to lead teams in product development and product marketing. This involves a number of things. First, the product manager shouldn't be afraid to admit ignorance. Even though most technical product managers do have significant backgrounds in their fields, chances are they don't have the technical skills of the existing engineers on the team. Second, it's important to know when to intervene. Although it's essential that the team members learn to work together, especially in the new product endeavors, the product manager still has ultimate responsibility for the success of the product line.

These skills are built over time. According to Bill Meserve:

> Beginning product managers with focused responsibilities need specific knowledge about the company's product and competitive offerings. As job experience and responsibility increase, the focus of skills building shifts to functional areas like financial analysis, promotion, pricing design, new-

---

Product Managers in the Electronics (continued)

---

product development and strategic selling. And when professional responsibilities progress to even higher levels, management skills become central. Product managers learn to build a team, achieve consensus, negotiate agreements, measure performance and handle personal relationships. Companies such as Allen-Bradley Co., 3M Co. and E.I. du Pont de Nemours & Co. supplement education with direct customer interaction, mentor relationships and cross-functional training to enhance product management skills.

Source: Adapted from Bill Meserve, "The Changing Role of Product Management," *Electronic Business*, 9 (January 1989): 143–146.

---

salespeople must be given an easy and efficient way to share market knowledge with product managers, and be motivated to do so. With the growth of sales forces equipped with laptop computers, bulletin boards and electronic mail (E-mail) can be significant tools in gaining market feedback. Fax lines, toll-free numbers, and traditional print mechanisms can also be used. Regardless of the method used to collect the information, a standard intelligence report form simplifies the process for both the salespeople and the product managers. Once market data is received, the product manager must recognize the salespeople for their contributions as well as demonstrate to the sales force that the information is being used to their advantage.

The development of sales forecasts is generally the domain of product managers, but forecasting frequently cannot be completed without the input of the sales force. Salespeople might be requested to estimate sales in their territories in total or by customer and/or product. If the information is broken down by account, it is likely to include an estimate of the probability of attainment. The forecast will be given to the regional or national sales manager, collated, and forwarded to the marketing department. The product manager would work in concert with the marketing analyst to arrive at a realistic forecast for the product line.

Communicating with Salespeople

On an operational level, product managers spend a moderate amount of time on the phone with salespeople and prospects. Sometimes the calls are requests for price adjustments or special deals that require product management approval or authorization. Other calls will be questions about product attributes. The more itemized the product fact book (see Chapter 8), the more efficient a product manager will be in providing the answers. Even if salespeople have received the information previously, it is often quicker and more efficient for them if the product manager provides the information on the spot.

That does not mean that the product manager should not also provide the sales force with written information. Salespeople should be informed of any product or marketing change that affects their relationships or negotiations with customers before the information reaches their customers! Mailgram, E-mail, fax, special delivery, and similar techniques are useful for high-priority information.

Many companies require product managers to spend a certain amount of time (e.g., 25–30 percent) making customer contacts, possibly through calls with salespeople. These sales calls provide an opportunity to learn more about the customer, or on some occasions to help close a sale. However, there must be clarity prior to the call about the specific role the product manager is expected to play.

Most of the operational activities will not appear on the marketing plan, although they might be part of annual performance objectives (e.g., percentage of time spent in the field). What should be included in the marketing plan are budgets for travel expenses, any special incentive programs (for spurring sales of products that aren't achieving objectives or for introducing new products), or any activities undertaken as part of territory redesign or sales force changes.

Sales Training

Sales force training can cover a variety of issues: sales skills, company data, product knowledge, and market and competitive intelligence. The effectiveness of training can be a significant factor in making a new product launch successful.[1] (See Chapter 10 for more on new-product launching.) Although teaching sales skills per se will not typically be part of a product manager's responsibilities, the product training does have to fit within the framework of the selling process, and the market and competitive intelligence has to be presented in support of this process.

As an example, assume that five elements are included in a company's standard sales training process: (1) planning, (2) establishing trust, (3) qualifying needs, (4) providing customized and visible solutions, and (5) building partnerships. The product training and the role of the product manager should fit into this process.

Planning

First, what information will help the salespeople in the function of planning? They need to know who is most likely to buy the product. Instead of describing the primary and secondary target markets, the product manager should profile the "ideal" account, suggesting specific customers, if appropriate. If noncustomers need to be cultivated, salespeople need to know the types of uses, applications, and functions appropriate for the product. For example, a company selling flat panel display screens might direct salespeople to engineers in specific industries that require a monitor with graphics clarity.

Both product managers and salespeople should understand the differences between key accounts, target accounts, and maintenance accounts (as well as, of course, "why bother?" accounts). Key accounts consist of the 20 percent of customers who account for 80 percent of gross profitability. Target accounts are those customers who form the competitors' key accounts, or they are significant prospects for a new product or service. Maintenance accounts may include existing small customers and possibly *future* strategic accounts.[2]

Establishing Trust

Second, how will the product manager help establish trust with the customer? If a new product is being introduced, the product manager has to demonstrate that the internal support systems are already in place, that the product has been tried and proven, and that customer orders can indeed be filled if sales are made. Promotional support aimed at "getting a foot in the door" of noncustomers can also be shared with salespeople, along with tips on effective use of support material.

Qualifying Needs

Third, what information about the customers must the salespeople obtain to qualify needs? What does the salesperson need to know about the prospect to determine the appropriateness of the sale? Customer satisfaction results from the best match between product benefits and customer needs. If the salespeople "successfully" sell to the wrong people or for the wrong applications, the revenue will be short-lived. Therefore, the product manager must provide customer-friendly questions that enable salespeople to assess the fit before closing the sale.

There should be questions about how prospects perform the function(s) provided by the product, what tolerances are required, what applications they would have for it now and in the future, and so on. The questions should not simply push the prospect toward a sale, but rather indicate whether the prospect has a true need for the product (thereby screening out inappropriate prospects). For example, a college textbook product manager responsible for a line of products to be sold to university professors will need to provide questions that assess teaching philosophy, level of rigor, and content preferences of the faculty, while the product manager selling flat panel display screens may need to determine whether the screen is used in bright sunlight or office light, whether the primary usage is text or graphics, and whether simple or complex software is involved.

Customizing Solutions

Fourth, how can salespeople use the answers from the preceding questions to develop customized and visible solutions for the account? This requires the product manager to look for creative ways to demonstrate a product's competitive edge. (See Part III for more on this subject.)

Building Partnerships

Fifth, what assurance is there that this product will increase the partnership already established between the customer and the salesperson? Customer partnerships require careful and timely follow-up to questions and problems. Salespeople expect the necessary support in installation, training, troubleshooting, and repair. Even though product managers may not have the hands-on abilities to handle all the activities, they still have the responsibility to be sure they get done. There-fore, their interactions with customers and product support services (as mentioned later in this chapter) will help salespeople cement long-term relationships with customers. (More information on working with the sales force as part of a new-product launch is presented in Chapter 10.)

Operations and Research and Development (R&D)

Product managers of both service products and manufactured products are dependent on operations to create the right product at the right price and deliver it at the right time for customers. Whether operations refers to underwriting, loan management, manufacturing, or logistics, a close working relationship is critical.

New-Product Development

Perhaps the most visible interaction a product manager will have with operations is during new-product development. The research and devel-opment department will need to assess technical feasibility; manufactur-ing will need to evaluate future efficiency and productivity; procurement might need to be involved with make-versus-buy decisions; and over-all capacity considerations will need to be taken into account. The role of the product manager will be to represent the voice of the customer, balancing corporate return on investment (ROI), customer satisfaction, and manufactured cost. Mutually acceptable standards for quality and customer service will need to be established so that manufacturing and marketing strategies are complementary rather than conflicting.

Strategic Interactions

The product manager can also be involved in strategy sessions with the operations function, separate from new-product development. During these sessions, the product manager will present marketplace problems and/or competitive moves that might trigger ideas for new products and highlight discussion on future capacity needs. This is also the time when product managers learn of technology looking for a market and are encouraged to think of ways to incorporate new technology into exist-ing or planned products in a way that is acceptable to the market. For example, when Ford first developed front-disc brakes, there was concern about how to introduce them into cars given that there would be an inevitable price impact. They decided to introduce them as an upscale option on expensive cars until the price could be driven low enough through mass production to be appropriate for any vehicle:

> The most important lesson was in marketing. Disc brakes were, in principle, not much more expensive to produce than drum brakes; they weren't made of gold. But we were going down the manufacturing learning curve, and were thus comparing costs with a very old design. We had to find a way to get the new brakes paid for without looking dumb.
>
> We solved the problem by choosing an expensive car where the customer would not care quite as much about price, making disc brakes an upscale option for the Lincoln. . . . Once production was automated, the price began to drop. Today, the cost difference between a disc brake and drum brake is minuscule.[3]

The product manager must work continuously with operations to improve and enhance the product line. This requires that a product manager have at least a basic understanding (if in a manufacturing environment) of material scrapped due to worker error, the time it takes to set up a production line, and other operations performance measures. In insurance, product managers may need to understand basic underwriting guidelines. In financial services, product managers may need knowledge of the secondary market for loans and various financial ratios.

Product managers are frequently involved with operations on cost-reduction projects. Because product managers are expected to bring market insights, they have to focus on ways of reducing costs that will not compromise the perceived value of a product. Cost reduction should not be fleeting. That is, care must be taken that cost savings are not temporary, with the inevitable result of other costs going up in the future.

Other operations-related activities a product manager might undertake include the following:

- leading synergy sessions to ensure that all functions are moving in the same direction;
- encouraging discussion of technological advancements that could affect future new products;
- establishing task forces to conduct value analysis on existing products;
- monitoring productivity improvements; and

- fostering teamwork to enhance productivity on an ongoing basis.

Customer and Product Support Services

Customer service as a function can exist in marketing, warehousing, sales, or some other department, depending on the organizational structure of the firm. The product manager should both gather information from customer service representatives (CSRs) on product performance and supply information to them to increase customer satisfaction with the product line. Part of the added value for many products is the service level provided by the company. The product manager has to ensure that the service standards are established, understood, and attainable by the service staff.

For service standards to be attainable, CSRs require training. Product managers might request support from the company's human resources function, include CSRs in the product training done for the sales force, and/or develop specific training for them. The more important service is as part of the product's competitive differentiation, the more important it is for product managers to take an active role in making sure the training happens.

The handling of warranties, for example, will require clarity among CSRs. If the warranty specifies thirty days and a complaint is received on the thirty-first day, what leeway do the CSRs have in deciding how to handle it? What leeway should they have?

Finance

Product managers must work with finance to achieve a balance between the way products are costed and the market price desired. Customers don't care what internal cost allocation mechanism a company uses to set a floor for pricing. Their concern is simply whether a product has sufficient value given the competitive alternatives available. Although all costs must be covered to remain profitable in the long term, contribution pricing in concert with market segmentation or product life cycle decisions can be valuable. For example, pharmaceutical companies use contribution pricing to determine how long to sell an old product once a new one has been introduced:

Often new drugs are introduced that are more effective or have fewer side effects than older drugs, but the older drug still may be marketed. . . . Then the price would fall. The company would discontinue the product when it no longer makes a contribution. It may discontinue sooner if it can use existing capacity to produce products with a higher contribution.[4]

Product managers must also rely on finance to provide line-item information for the budget, pro forma income statement, and/or product balance sheet. By negotiating what information is critical for decision making, both functions can operate more effectively. The relevance of specific costs varies by situation and depends on the decision to be made. Product managers who can work with finance to ferret out the appropriate costs will be in a better position to make the right decisions.

Marketing Communications

Whether dealing with an internal advertising department or an external ad agency, a product manager needs a general understanding of promotional alternatives to be able to evaluate copy and media recommendations effectively. Typically, product managers will determine what positioning they want for their products, and the communication of that positioning will be left to the functional specialists. Product managers need to describe the target market they are trying to reach as precisely as possible so that the advertising groups can use that information to select the appropriate media and media vehicles.

If there are several product managers working for a company, they must consider the relative merits of advertising the company as a whole versus positioning the various products independently of the company. A number of companies are moving to an umbrella approach to branding, in which the company name, reputation, and position are being emphasized as much as or more than the individual brand. The product managers and advertising specialists can discuss the relative merits of each option and come to an agreement prior to investing heavily in advertising.

If a product manager can choose between an in-house and an external agency, which one should be selected? Obviously there are several factors to consider. An external agency can be preferable for the product manager who needs an outside viewpoint, faces resource constraints internally making it difficult to meet deadlines, and/or wants to take advantage of an agency's potential for mass media buying. On the other hand, an internal department might be the right decision if the product manager needs to capitalize on the expertise resulting from knowlege of a very specialized market, has the necessary skill in-house, and wants more control over the total process.[5]

There are several questions involved in agency selection: (1) What types of promotion, in addition to advertising, might need to be done? Many companies, particularly in business-to-business situations, need direct-mail, lead-generation programs, trade show coverage, or special sales promotion techniques. (2) Does the agency understand the target and have the appropriate talent to speak the language? This does not mean that a technical message needs to be written by a technical person. In fact, a technical slant may be completely wrong in cases where the focus should be on benefits rather than features. However, the copywriter needs to understand how to translate features into appropriate benefits for the customer. (3) Should a large or small agency be hired? Typically, the most effective arrangement is for the client size to match the agency size, and it is better to be the big fish in a small pond than the reverse. However, there may be exceptions, particularly where innovative new products are concerned. (4) Will the agency be expected to help with general marketing, Internet marketing, research, and/or strategic planning? If so, this might narrow the pool of potential agencies.

Marketing Research

Although product managers must necessarily have good information on the market and the competition, they are not usually experts in data collection and analysis. That's why much customer research is farmed out to either internal research departments or external research agencies. Product managers can also take advantage of the marketing research supplied by many advertising agencies or even some media publications.

Customers

Customer contact is an expectation for virtually all product managers. Consumer-goods brand managers usually reach customers through focus groups and other research techniques. Business-to-business product managers are more likely to contact customers while on calls with salespeople, although marketing research is growing in importance for that group as well. The critical point in meeting with customers is to be open to both shortfalls in existing products and long-term future needs. As difficult as it is, product managers must visualize innovations that anticipate and satisfy unmet needs.

Checklist: Fitting Product Managers into the Organization

✓ To be most effective as a product manager, focus on being a generalist who can accomplish work through other people and functional departments.

✓ Position yourself with the sales force so that you're viewed as neither strictly sales support nor corporate dictator.

✓ Understand how your activities fit into the sales process.

✓ Be prepared to represent the voice of the customer in meetings with operations and R & D and to demonstrate at least a minimum understanding of operational techniques and standards.

✓ Don't be afraid to question and critique the work of your internal or external advertising agency.

✓ Allocate a significant portion of the time you spend with customers gathering information on *future* product needs and applications.

Case One[1]

Heavyweight Product Managers

DURING THE 1980s, product managers began to appear at more and more automotive companies. The motivation for this change was the growth in international competition (today more than twenty auto companies are global), the increasing complexity of the products, and more demanding, sophisticated customers. Product managers (called "large product leaders" at Honda and "program managers" at Ford) were challenged to create not only functionally superior cars, but also cars that are distinctive and embody a certain personality or "feel" consistent with future customer needs.

This last aspect, bringing in the customer, is where the product manager is most critical. The auto companies had previously used matrix structures, coordinator committees, cross-functional teams, and other structural mechanisms to improve product development, but these were frequently inward-focused and did not anticipate future customer desires. External integration is an important and difficult task of the development process. Unless a company makes a deliberate effort to integrate customers into the development process, it is likely to create products that are technologically advanced and offer good value but fall short with sophisticated customers.

Ford's "Program Manager" Structure

Ford is one company that had success with this organizational concept. The Taurus, introduced in 1985, was designed to be a family vehicle with sophisticated European styling, handling, and ride. Its success was due to Team Taurus, the cross-functional group responsible for this product. The effectiveness of the team became the catalyst for organizational change at Ford. Shortly thereafter, it formalized the "program manager" concept that evolved out of the Taurus experience.

The structure reinforced cross-functional integration at both the strategy and operational levels. In particular, marketing people (led by the program manager) began to meet directly with designers and engineers. Previously, their involvement had been through reports and memos. The program managers themselves were given greater responsibility for product planning and layout.

As this organizational structure continued to grow, the strength of the program manager position increased, as did the effectiveness of the product-development process. Several products that were developed out of this structure followed the market success of the Taurus: the Lincoln Continental, the Thunderbird Super Coupe, the Probe, and the Explorer.

As time went on, Ford management discovered that integrated development required more than a cross-functional team. It became clear that simply assigning a project leader to a team did not guarantee product integrity. The effectiveness of the program manager was the missing link.

When markets were relatively stable, companies could achieve product integrity through strong functional organizations. The ability to achieve superior product integrity now depends on the leadership of the product manager. The product manager becomes the thread tying all the pieces together, filling in the gaps and ensuring that the final product is consistent with the original product-customer concept, with a special effort placed on understanding what customer wants will be at the time a new product is introduced rather than what they are right now. This person must be able to understand

- what the product does (performance and technical functions);
- what the product is (configuration, component technologies);
- who the product serves (target market); and
- what the product means to customers (character, personality, image).

Characteristics of Heavyweight Product Managers

Of course, not all product managers provide the same level of effectiveness. Kim Clark and Takahiro Fujimoto, in their *Harvard Business Review* article "The Power of Product Integrity," differentiate between "heavyweight" product managers and "their lighter-weight counterparts." According to their research in the automotive industry, many product managers are functional workers rather than cross-functional leaders. They lack influence outside of product engineering, have little or no contact with working-level engineers or with marketing, and act primarily as facilitators and coordinators. As a result, they spend much of their time going to meetings, reading reports, and writing memos.

Heavyweight product managers, on the other hand, function as the product's general manager. Clark and Fujimoto explain:

> In addition to concept-related duties, the responsibilities that come with the job include: coordinating production and sales as well as engineering; coordinating the entire project from concept to market; signing off on specification, cost-target, layout and major component choices; and maintaining direct contact with existing and potential customers. Heavyweight product managers have a broad knowledge of the product and process engineering required to develop an entire vehicle. Years of experience with the companies give their words weight and increase their influence with people over whom they have no formal authority.

Honda's "large product leader" is such a position. It combines the generation of a strong product concept with the ability to carry it through development to the final product experience for the end-customer.

Honda Accord: Maintaining Product Integrity

When the product manager for the Honda Accord began the third-generation design, he was challenged with maintaining the concept "man maximum, machine minimum" throughout the development process while still repositioning the Accord to fit future customer expectations. Starting with a series of small-group brainstorming sessions, the product leader and his team decided to personify the car's message to consumers with the image of "a rugby player in a business suit." The next step was to break this image down into specific attributes of a car. Five sets of key words were chosen: *open-minded, friendly communication, tough spirit, stress-free,* and *love forever. Tough spirit* was translated into maneuverability in difficult conditions. *Love forever* translated into long-term customer satisfaction. *Stress-free* led to efforts in noise and vibration reduction.

To capture all of these elements was a challenge for the Accord design team. In an effort to allow maximum space and visibility for the occupants, a low engine hood and a larger-than-usual front window were part of the design. Unfortunately the large window meant that the car could get uncomfortably hot in the summer unless there was a large air conditioner, requiring a large engine. And the large engine was contrary to the desire for a low engine hood.

Rather than allowing this to develop into an either-or decision, the product leader reminded the team to look at their work through future customers' eyes and to maintain the integrity of the initial concept. The result was the development of a new engine that was both compact and powerful.

As the Honda example shows, being market-oriented is a critical role of the talented product manager. However, as Clark and Fujimoto also point out, it requires more than that:

> It begins with customers, to be sure, since the best concept developers invariably supplement the cooked information they get from marketing specialists with raw data they gather themselves. But strong product concepts also include a healthy measure of what we call "market imagination": they encompass what customers say they want and what the concept's creators imagine customers will want three or more years into the future. Remembering that customers know only existing products and existing technologies, they avoid the trap of being too close to customers and of designing products that will be out-of-date before they are even manufactured.

The product manager must juggle numerous details and ensure that the subtleties of a product concept are not lost in development and marketing. Although creating product and marketing plans is part of this effort, an essential task is the interpersonal communication of the somewhat intangible ideas. Daily communication with functional engineering departments during the design phase and with plant personnel during the development phase is a necessary role of the product manager. Similarly, product managers test-drive the vehicles and continually strive to attain strong product integrity:

> The product manager's job touches every part of the new product process. Indeed, heavyweight product managers have to be "multilingual," fluent in the languages of customers, marketers, engineers, and designers. On one side, this means being able to translate an evocative concept like the pocket rocket into specific targets like "maximum speed 250 kilometers per hour" and "drag coefficient less than 0.3" that detail-oriented engineers can easily grasp. On the other side, it means being able to assess and communicate what a "0.3 drag coefficient" will mean to the customers.

Outstanding product management organizations depend on the consistency between the formal and informal organizational structure. Honda demonstrated this consistency in some important ways. Communication lines were open and direct rather than indirect. Functional specialists were respected but not put on a pedestal. And the product concept was infused through the product team.

General Motors: Making Improvements

The lack of a heavyweight product manager can detract from a firm's ability to capture product integrity. When General Motors (GM) introduced the Allante in 1987, analysts felt they rushed to introduction rather than first working out the bugs. The car was attractive but not necessarily distinctive. It was too small for core Cadillac buyers and lacked the necessary quality to lure import buyers. In other words, it was not externally integrated.

GM's process of product development has been quite different from that of Honda and Chrysler. While those companies place the decisions about a vehicle in the hands of an autonomous team, GM traditionally preferred to preserve the power of functional departments. However, even at GM there has been a shift to a more unified approach. Kathleen Kerwin, in her *Business Week* article "GM's Aurora," discusses how the development of the Oldsmobile Aurora initiated changes in terms of cross-functional cooperation and increased input from the customer:

> [The process of developing the Aurora] meant that the GM design engineers in Flint joined efforts with Oldsmobile's marketing group in Lansing and GM factory managers at the Lake Orion (Michigan) plant. In cases [such as this] where the various teams have a sense of common purpose, the results can be impressive.
>
> At the very least, Aurora is a sign that GM is finally listening to its customers. The No. 1 carmaker had long made a habit of ignoring customer input or delaying market research until the final stages of car development, when it was too late to make changes. By contrast Aurora's development team consulted extensively with consumer focus groups even before the first designs were drawn. Now, the "Voice of the Customer" has become GM's new rallying cry.

Like Ford and Honda, Oldsmobile struggled with product integrity in its work on the Aurora. The vehicle was designed as a niche car, intended to attract affluent, quality-conscious baby boomers. In discussing the car with potential customers, a nameless characteristic kept emerging as an important feature: something about German cars that connoted security and that protected drivers from bumps and jolts. The design team determined this came from a rigid body structure. Unfortunately, providing this rigidity without sacrificing the smooth, flowing lines of the design was a challenge. To accomplish both objectives simultaneously, the engineers devised a way to spray molten silicon bronze into the roof seam instead of using conventional welding. The result was a distinctive car that retained the original concept through the design process.

Product Managers in Other Industries

Heavyweight product managers in other industries have some of the same characteristics as in the automotive industry. As Jean LeGrand states in her article in *Bankers Magazine*, "A Product in Need of Management," a successful product manager in the banking industry "must be a senior-level professional, widely regarded in the profession." This individual must understand "complex portfolio management programs and such quantitative models as cost accounting and return on equity (ROE) computations." And, as in the automotive industry, the position requires market knowledge and the ability to translate technical concepts into customer-appropriate terms.

In fast-moving consumer goods (FMCG) companies, product managers (frequently called "brand managers") are less likely to have industry experience, but rather have strong management and marketing skills, typically requiring an MBA. They are expected to create a strong brand recognition for their products through their ability to command respect, maintain momentum throughout a product-related project, and motivate everyone toward the same goal. As with heavyweight product managers in other industries, the FMCG brand manager must strive for and champion product integrity.

4

Product manager.com

Technology in its many forms has, and will continue to have, an escalating impact on the role of product managers. E-mail, fax, and video-conference technologies have shortened the communication time between product managers and their constituencies. (This has benefited product managers requesting information, but has also made response time to requests shorter and more demanding.) Improved manufacturing and distribution processes have heightened competitive maneuvers to the realm of hypercompetition. The Internet has provided opportunities to reach new customers, but it has also complicated brand strategies and channel issues. The explosion of information technologies has touched everything from database management to E-commerce.

A product manager from an industrial component company stated in an E-mail message to me:

> Technology is the key that unlocks the door of progress. We as product managers use any software or hardware that our companies can afford. The advancement of technology has enabled one person to do the work that in the past took at least two or three people to do. We are able to keep in constant contact with both customers and coworkers by E-mail. We take and place orders through secure web connections. We are working toward a paperless workplace. My opinion is that if you are not proficient in the use of the technology available you may not fail now but you will fail eventually.[1]

Four areas of technology are explored in this chapter: (1) communications, (2) research, (3) internal systems, and (4) web marketing and E-commerce.

Communications

One of the most obvious areas of technological impact is the explosion of E-mail, fax, teleconferencing, videoconferencing, and other tools to expedite communication. Most product managers agree that E-mail is a blessing and a curse at the same time. On the positive side, it enables people to send messages at any time, twenty-four hours a day, to any place in the world. Product managers can use it to gather information from internal team members (e.g., salespeople, marketing, product development, and support); communicate with customers, reach distribution partners in Europe, Latin America, South Africa, and the Pacific Rim; and acknowledge prospects. The ability to respond is convenient, since it simply requires pressing the "send" button to execute. Numerous people can receive the information simultaneously with virtually no marginal cost. Therein lies the downside of E-mail. Because it has become so easy for numerous people to be copied on a message or response, it can create another source of "information overload." Also, since many E-communications between product managers and salespeople involve singular customer or product problems, broadcasting them to numerous people can result in a "groupthink" phenomenon causing the problems to appear bigger than they actually are.

Faxing, similar to E-mail, allows twenty-four-hour message communication. The quality of the printed page may not always be as good as that of top-of-the line electronic messages, but not all customers have the ability to download Web materials or access E-mail attachments. Since facsimiles are more established technology, a higher percentage of customers will be likely to have the appropriate equipment. Faxing will continue to be an important part of the communication between sellers and buyers for the near future.

Teleconferencing is another way for product managers to communicate at a distance with more than one individual. It enables product managers to have three-way links, for example, serving as a liaison between sales and internal functions such as manufacturing or product support. This can be an effective tool for product development and marketing meetings. Although timing is an issue for international tele-conferences, it provides a means of sharing information without the expense of global travel. Some product managers are using this technology for tele-focus groups with customers. One particular software product manger, for example, has contracted with a marketing research firm to hold four tele-focus groups from different global regions to assess the market potential for a new product idea.

Videoconferencing is becoming quite common for global companies. Product managers with global brands can link with various country representatives to improve the effectiveness of marketing strategies in various world regions through short-term training, idea generation, or question-and-answer sessions. Videoconferencing is still quite expensive and is used less frequently than teleconferencing, but usage will increase as costs go down over time.

Regardless of the technology tools used for communication purposes, product mangers need to remember the importance of face-to-face contact with internal team members, salespeople, and customers. Sometimes a phone call, a personal visit, or even a short handwritten note can be more effective than technology in getting buy-in and results. As one product manager said, "it's important not to kill flies with a hammer."

Research

The Internet and the Web provide several resources for product managers to use in conducting marketing research. By way of definition, the Internet is a network of computer networks—a way of linking business, government, and other networks to one another electronically. Initially started as a text-based system, the introduction of the World Wide Web (or www.) now allows transmission of graphical bits of data as well.

A product manager from a software company stated, "I use the Web daily to perform competitive research and look for new product ideas. I really don't know how I survived prior to using the Web."[2] Another product manager from a music equipment company also finds several uses of the Internet:

> I search for end-user opinions by going to DejaNews (www.dejanews
> .com) and searching the news groups for relevant discussions. Also,

I can visit my competitors' websites to obtain product specs and search for the "street price" of various products on-line. We have a company compile the information from returned warranty cards into a database that we can search to learn more about our customer base. We also offer on-line product registration for certain products.[3]

There are several tools for accessing market intelligence using the Web, as indicated in Figure 4.1. Some are free, some require registration (with or without fees), and others offer a combination of some "free" information, with fees required to access more detailed data. For general content searching of new ideas, customer issues, and trends, MetaCrawler, DejaNews, and ForumOne are example sources. Meta-Crawler is a mega search engine that searches several search engines simultaneously. It reduces overlaps and redundancies in the search process. DejaNews is an archive of discussion (usenet) groups. ForumOne is a search engine of Web-based discussion groups. The two latter sources can be somewhat overwhelming, since several discussions can be extraneous to your product, but unique ideas can emerge. To obtain specific information more consistently, you might try prioritizing topics in the news to create a variation of an on-line clipping service using NewsPage.

For market data (e.g., analytical data on segment sizes by SIC or NAICS classification), the U.S. Census Bureau is a good starting point. Although much of the information cannot be obtained on-line, the website describes the types of censuses available and provides examples of how to use the data. Several sites can be accessed from the home page, including The Statistical Abstract of the United States and The State and Metropolitan Area Data Book. The Bureau of Labor Statistics website provides links to the eleven principal federal statistical agencies, as well as to the official government-sponsored statistical services of several countries. Another tool, published by The Population Reference Bureau, organizes information by state as well as information general to all states. Sometimes the best sources of market information are trade and industry associations. If you are unaware of specific associations and websites, a place to start looking is the Internet Public Library (IPL) Associations on the Internet. This is a page of the Internet Public Library website with a collection of over eleven hundred (as of August 1999) Internet sites providing information about a wide variety of associations.

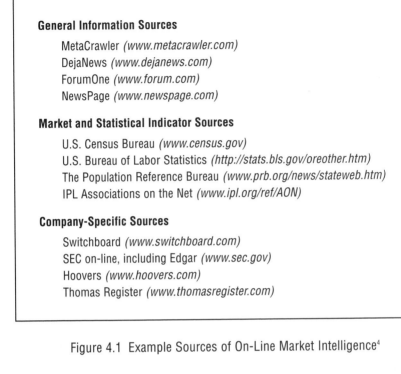

General Information Sources

MetaCrawler *(www.metacrawler.com)*
DejaNews *(www.dejanews.com)*
ForumOne *(www.forum.com)*
NewsPage *(www.newspage.com)*

Market and Statistical Indicator Sources

U.S. Census Bureau *(www.census.gov)*
U.S. Bureau of Labor Statistics *(http://stats.bls.gov/oreother.htm)*
The Population Reference Bureau *(www.prb.org/news/stateweb.htm)*
IPL Associations on the Net *(www.ipl.org/ref/AON)*

Company-Specific Sources

Switchboard *(www.switchboard.com)*
SEC on-line, including Edgar *(www.sec.gov)*
Hoovers *(www.hoovers.com)*
Thomas Register *(www.thomasregister.com)*

Figure 4.1 Example Sources of On-Line Market Intelligence[4]

For company-specific data on competitors, the best places to start are your competitors' websites. They frequently contain information on new products and suggest positioning strategies. If you don't know a site address, you might try Switchboard, a telephone, E-mail, or Web directory. Some information on competitors and competitor site addresses may also be available through industry trade associations, as mentioned in the previous paragraph. In addition, there are a handful of industry *portals* (sites to connect buyers and sellers) that have emerged with extensive lists of suppliers. PaperExchange, for example, includes a directory of suppliers to the paper industry. For financial information on the competition, the SEC is a starting point; you can use the Edgar database to look up common SEC forms for a designated company. Hoovers is a commercial organization that provides company and product information on numerous firms. In addition, Hoovers publishes industry overviews that may provide useful information and additional industry website links. The Thomas Register of American Manufacturers provides product information on a variety of firms.

Internal Systems

One of the ongoing challenges of product management is the need to sort through, analyze, and synthesize large amounts of data. Organizing competitor and customer data into convenient formats for decision-making requires significant time and effort. Most existing companies are mired in a mix of different databases, computer systems, and functional processes, making integration difficult. At the same time, customer demands and competitive pressures are escalating the need for this level of integration. A financial institution, for example, may have different databases for checking accounts, savings accounts, CDs, and other financial vehicles. Without the ability to integrate these systems, customers receive separate statements for each of their accounts.

In many situations, several product managers "share" the same customers. If information is maintained simply on a transaction or product basis, there is no repository of common customer data to learn from and grow in an effort to serve customers better than the competition does. This type of integrated system is a necessary prerequisite to effective E-commerce.

Having a good database on customers and being able to use it effectively is becoming increasingly significant for companies in today's competitive environment. Various terms have been used to describe this process, including data mining, customer asset management (CAM), and customer relationship management (CRM). Data mining refers to the process of extracting knowledge about a particular topic (in this case, customers) from a compiled database. CAM and CRM more specifically refer to marketing and sales automation or software that facilitates a firm's ability to build relationships with customers. Product managers and salespeople have historically managed customer relationships quite well, but now there is software that links the whole company together to manage customers.[5] The idea behind CRM is to provide a holistic approach to using customer information throughout the company.

The majority of companies have websites today, most have intranets, and a growing number are doing business with customers and suppliers via extranets. However, the individual components may not be used as effectively as they could be, and the components are generally not linked well to one another. The processes and software used to link databases together not only improve interactions with customers, but also provide the foundation for E-commerce and broad-based customer relationship management:

> [I]n order to do a good job with your website, you're going to need to integrate it tightly into many of your company's back-end systems. Ideally, you'll want to design a generalizable integration strategy for all those applications, not a piecemeal approach. Second, you'll begin to recognize that you could use many of the same features you design into your website to enable customers to help themselves using Touch-Tone telephones, kiosks, or hand-held devices. You can even use much of the information and streamlined processes in the call centers where your sales and service people are interacting with customers on the phone. And you can reuse a lot of the processes and information you develop for your end customers to serve your channel partners.[6]

Companies are looking for ways to use the intranet for *knowledge management*. Knowledge management, in general, refers to a corporate-wide *program* or *process* for organizing, filtering, sharing, and retaining key corporate data as an asset. Whether E-mail, GroupWare (such as LOTUS Notes), data mining, or other approaches are used, intranets are becoming a forum for discussing ideas, sharing new information about competitors and customers, and comparing notes on product development projects. Product managers can and should work with their information technology group to evolve their intranets into tools to enable market-driven decisions. Many experts are confirming David Packard's ubiquitous quote that "marketing is too important to be left to the marketing department," by highlighting the importance of this information-sharing.

In small organizations where product and customer discussions take place informally on an ongoing basis, information is continually shared and intellectual capital can thereby grow into a competitive edge. As corporations have evolved into massive global structures, product managers may find it necessary to replace some of the face-to-face sharing of expertise of the past by using technology as the "virtual office water-cooler" of the twenty-first century. The pharmaceutical firm Wyeth-Ayerst has realized the importance of this phenomenon:

> Wyeth-Ayerst has discovered remarkable benefits from the implementation of a global knowledge sharing database. Benefits that range from quantifiable increases in market share through the adoption of

successful business strategies across the sales organization, to the development of product launch models which have taken into account the organization's most successful practices. They have found that one of the most interesting comments received from employees who utilize the knowledge sharing database is the realization that, no matter their location, when they go to work each day, they firmly believe that their ability to access a repository of company-wide knowledge and expertise provides them a distinct and significant competitive advantage.[7]

Similar knowledge sharing can occur between companies through use of extranets. A firm can, for example, link up with another firm's intranet to allow authorized people to access inventory records, review sales information, and/or order electronically (a Web-based version of EDI, electronic data interchange).

Web Marketing and E-Commerce

Establishing an Internet presence, creating a Web marketing plan, preparing for electronic commerce, or some similar phrase describes the final technological challenge for the product manager. Planning for this challenge should include establishing goals, defining the target audience, preparing for start-up issues, designing content, integrating the electronic media with internal and external company systems, deciding how to track effectiveness, and assigning responsibility for maintaining the site(s).

Goals

Let's start with the first issue regarding the goals for your Internet or Web strategy. Typically, when companies get started in E-commerce, their first-generation website consists almost exclusively of "brochureware" or focuses on establishing a corporate image. This is a logical and necessary first step, as it can provide customers and prospects with contact information as well as basic product and service data. The question of whether to *sell* electronically depends on the industry you are in as well as your firm's desire to maintain solid relations with its channel; but, in general, Web strategies are moving in that direction. Therefore, E-mail addresses and order-entry capabilities should be included in the website.

The Issues of product manager.com

Goals: information, image, sales
Target audience: demographics, firmographics, connection capabilities
Start-up issues: budget, technologies required, domain name, promotion
Content: information, interactivity, links
Integration: style manual, customer-contact processes, databases
Evaluation and tracking: technological efficiency, marketing effectiveness
Maintenance: who, how frequently

Figure 4.2 Planning Issues for Web Marketing

Target Audience

Although many people may view the site, it should be designed with the *target audience* in mind. For consumer audiences, consider the standard demographics such as age, sex, income, occupation, and interests. For business audiences, focus on industry type, function, management position, and similar characteristics. For both groups, pay attention to the technological capabilities of the equipment they are likely to be using. If the site is being designed primarily to link with resellers (e.g., dealers), don't overlook the end buyers as a *secondary market.*

Start-Up Issues

Starting up the process requires resources, including technological capabilities, people, and money. It also requires a decision on the domain name as well as marketing communication activities to increase awareness and pull traffic to the site. The domain name (amazon.com, or ama.org) refers to the name registered by your information systems (IS) department. It is often the name of the firm or organization, and occasionally the name of the brand or product group. If there are several names by which customers know you, or if misspellings are common, it's a good idea to register several domain names. Once companies have a Web presence, customers have to be notified of the address. This can be done through advertising, press releases, E-mail, reciprocal links to other sites, direct mail, or other standard promotional methods. It's also a good idea for letterhead, business cards, and other corporate communication devices to carry the website address.

Content

For business-to-business marketers, website content can be critical. On-line product literature can be invaluable as long as it is current and accurate. Be sure that all product managers use standard templates for creating separate web pages, and keep the pages short. Update product news on a weekly, if not daily, basis, and print dates on all pages to identify when they were last updated. Use E-mail to inform salespeople, channel members, and customers when significant product changes are made.

Websites should incorporate interactivity and "stickiness" to encourage customers to return to the site and stay longer once there. The Birdseye website (www.birdseye.com/exchange.html), for example, facilitates a recipe exchange. The results are increased traffic, increased return visits, more consumers bookmarking the site, and an enhanced image for Birdseye.[8]

Integration

The Web strategy should be integrated to other marketing strategies and tactics. Many companies develop style manuals to carry a consistent identity through all media. Permission marketing, customization, and the "stickiness" mentioned in the last paragraph require that the website be linked with a solid database. (See feature Success Stories on the Web.) For example, by linking the website with a customer database, it is possible to acknowledge key events in the customer's life (e.g., a birthday) and accommodate personal preferences.

Will your branding or positioning need to change? Many experts expected the importance of brands to decrease with the growth of E-commerce, since buyers would be able to search out the best values to fit their needs. However, that may not always be true, since brands simplify the search process, build trust, and communicate a known level of quality. Some research has shown, in fact, that many customers have difficulty finding categories of products and services using search engines, and therefore have the tendency to turn to recognized brands.[9]

Success Stories on the Web

Companies are realizing that the Web is not a stand-alone marketing tool. It has to be integrated into an overall marketing communications, marketing, and channel strategy to be fully effective. Eddie Bauer, for example, uses its catalog, website, and retail stores to complement each other. The catalog promotes the on-line services and the website informs customers they can take products back to one of the stores if they are not satisfied. Store register receipts list the Web address.

Saturn's website enables customers to choose options for a new car and order on-line. This aspect of the website was portrayed humorously in a television commercial showing a college student using the Internet to order a Saturn as easily as ordering a pizza. The television commercial tripled visitors to the website.

Some companies use extranets and/or links to the intranets of key customers. Dell, for example, has established its Premier Page program. When it wins a customer with more than four hundred employees, it builds that customer a Premier Page, often linked to the customer's intranet. This makes it convenient for approved employees to go on-line to configure PCs, pay for them, and track delivery. Bayer, for example, has a leasing contract with Dell. Its Premier Page therefore links all the people who need to keep track of twenty-thousand leased PCs, and it regularly generates lease-management reports.

Pitney Bowes has established an extranet for its suppliers. Realizing that many smaller suppliers cannot afford electronic data interchange (EDI) software or massive enterprise resource planning (ERP) programs to forecast and manage inventory, Pitney Bowes created a low-cost link to its own ERP system. Now suppliers can see how many of their products Pitney has on hand and how many it will need for the next twelve months. Pitney updates its VendorSite weekly, and will start daily updates soon.

BP Amoco is testing a strategy to bring the Internet to its customers via its gas stations. It is expected to "turn gasoline pumps into Internet-connected kiosks" that will provide information (advertising) to

Success Stories on the Web (continued)

consumers as well as send E-mail to corporate headquarters when the pumps need servicing. This may provide the opportunity to offer special incentives to loyal customers.

Source: Condensed from David Bank, "BP Amoco to Unveil Deal with Tokheim to Supply Pumps with Web Browsers," *Wall Street Journal* (August 17, 1999): B6; De'Ann Weimer, "Can I Try (Click) that Blouse (Drag) in Blue?" *Business Week* (November 1998): 86; Ellen Neuborne and Robert D. Hof, "Branding on the Net," *Business Week* (November 1998): 76–86; and Eryn Brown et. al., "9 Ways to Win on the Web," *Fortune* (May 24, 1999): 112–125.

Evaluation and Tracking

The definition of "effectiveness" on the Web is still a bit elusive. Most experts agree that effectiveness has to be measured beyond counting the number of "hits" a website receives. However, this can be one criterion if your goal is primarily to increase awareness and spread your brand identity. Other criteria could include the length of time (on average) people spend at your site, the number of times customers or prospects return, direct sales, leads connecting through E-mail or an 800 number connected to the site, or requests for free information discussed on-line. You may also want to track the technological efficiency of your site using services such as www.websitegarage.com or www.netmechanic.com.

Maintenance

One of the most important (and frequently overlooked) issues involved in successful E-commerce is assigning responsibility for continual updating and maintenance of the website and related components. It is not uncommon for the entire budget to be "blown" during start-up without reserves for the salaries and time required to keep information current and to respond to customers. Product managers need to ensure that product, pricing, promotional, and related marketing data are kept up to date, and that distributors, customers, and salespeople are aware of changes that are added to the website. In other words, don't rely on the website alone to inform the necessary parties when you have changes to your product line.

Checklist: Making Technology Work for You

✓ Use E-mail selectively to reach the right people without causing "information overload" to everyone else.

✓ Experiment with teleconferencing tools to get data from customers as well as salespeople.

✓ Test new sites for competitive and market data, then bookmark those best suited to your product and industry.

✓ Learn about customer relationship management and the software or databases available to help you.

✓ Establish goals before jumping into E-commerce.

✓ Develop standard templates for product managers to use in creating separate Web pages for their product or product line.

✓ Update product news on a frequent (perhaps weekly) basis.

✓ Link the website to your customer database and internal systems.

✓ Assign responsibility to guarantee that your website is updated and maintained on an ongoing basis.

✓ Don't wait for customers, distributors, or salespeople to access your site when significant changes are made. Call or E-mail them directly.

Part II

PLANNING SKILLS FOR PRODUCT MANAGERS

One of the primary planning documents or tools that the product manager develops cooperatively with others in the company is the annual marketing plan for the product line. The planning process starts with an examination of current conditions to search for problems and opportunities for the product(s). After the problems and opportunities are identified and synthesized, a statement of direction for the next fiscal year is provided through sales and marketing objectives.

Finally, an action program is established that clarifies the strategies and tactics required to achieve the stated objectives. These strategies and tactics might encompass all of the traditional components of marketing, including a refinement of the target market; product changes and/or deletions; modifications in pricing; expansion/contraction or changes among distributors, dealers, and retailers; and improvements in marketing communication approaches. Commitment to follow through the strategies and tactics must be obtained from the respective functional areas in the company.

Part II discusses a process that product managers can use in their annual planning activities and presents a format for the annual product marketing plan.

5

The Product Marketing Planning Process

DAVID PACKARD OF Hewlett-Packard once said that marketing is "too important to be left to the marketing department." In other words, marketing is more than a job or a function; it's a philosophy about doing business. It's the recognition that customers form impressions about a company not only by the absolute quality of its products but also by a host of other factors. Customers want a product that addresses their specific needs. They want to be treated well by the seller's employees. They want to feel comfortable that the price they are paying reflects the perceived value of what they are buying. They want the process of buying to be easy and straightforward. That is all part of marketing—building a business around satisfying current and future market needs. Product managers play a formal role in this process through the development and execution of annual marketing plans for their products or product lines.

The planning process should cover three fundamental questions:

- Where are you now? (Background analysis, covered in Chapters 5 and 6)
- Where do you want to go? (Synthesis, covered in Chapter 7)
- How can you get there? (Action program, covered in Chapter 7)

Table 5.1 shows the types of information that make up each part of the process. This chapter covers the fundamental steps involved in the

Where are you now?	I. Background Analysis
	Business assessment
	Market analysis
	Competitive analysis
	Performance history
	Trend dynamics
Where do you want to go?	II. Synthesis
	Problems and opportunities
	Sales forecasts/goals
	Product objectives
	Positioning strategy
How can you get there?	III. Action Program
	Summary of background analysis and synthesis
	Target market
	Product strategy
	Pricing strategy
	Advertising strategy
	Promotion strategy
	Field sales strategy
	Distribution strategy
	Product support
	Training requirements
	Marketing research requirements
	Financial summary
	Schedules

Table 5.1 The Product Marketing Planning Process

process of planning. The next chapter provides tips on developing a product plan, ending with a sample outline and profit and loss statement.

Background Analysis: Where Are You Now?

The background analysis answers the question, "Where are you now?" and is the analytical part of the planning process that should precede

Figure 5.1 Business Assessment: Hierarchy of Strategies

development of the product plan. It includes a business assessment, a market analysis, a competitive analysis, a performance history, and an examination of trend dynamics.

Business Assessment

The first part of the business assessment is determining the vision and strategy of the overall company. (See Figure 5.1 Business Assessment: Hierarchy of Strategies and Figure 9.1 Assessing Your Company's Strategic IQ.) The vision is the mental picture of what the company will be in the future: the products it will offer and the markets it will serve. The corporate and divisional strategies are the general plans to move toward the vision. The product plans and marketing tactics should be consistent with the vision and strategies and move the company closer to superior customer satisfaction. The vision and corporate strategies are broad, with a focus on developing and leveraging core competencies. The product-specific strategies and tactics focus on customer-specific needs. (See Worksheet 5.1.)

The vision should highlight the core capabilities the company has or is willing to develop. For example, Komatsu, a Japanese manufacturer of earth-moving equipment, had a vision of beating Caterpillar. The strategies specified the skills it needed to acquire and the products

1. Describe the corporate vision, strategies, and core competencies that might affect the product programs.

2. List the strengths and weaknesses of the company that could directly affect the product or product line.

   Strengths:

   Weaknesses:

3. Describe the role your product/line plays in accomplishing the corporate strategy.

Worksheet 5.1 Business Assessment

it needed to develop to move toward that vision.[1] (See feature Komatsu's Long-Term Marketing Challenge.)

The business assessment also looks at the general culture of the company, the strengths that provide the core competence, the weaknesses that must be minimized, and the role a product/line plays in accomplishing the corporate strategy. The culture refers to the way a company operates: its philosophies, management style, and structure. A product manager cannot impact the culture in the short term but must rather understand and attempt to work within the culture. Example philosophies include the innovative, fast-paced organization and the conservative, "blue-chip" organization. The management style could be autocratic or democratic, with a resulting impact on a product manager's effectiveness.

There are several questions to ask as part of the business assessment to help identify key strengths and weaknesses of management, core competencies, the planning process, and other functional areas.

Management

1. Who are the actual movers and shakers of the company? Which ones should be part of a new-product venture?

2. Who is responsible for the budgeting process?

3. Does the company have any unusual business practices that are different from the competition?

Distinctive Competencies

1. What capabilities are the core of the firm's reason for being?

2. Are the various products leveraging these competencies effectively? (See Chapter 9 for further discussion.)

3. How can product managers leverage the capabilities of other parts of the company?

The Planning Process

1. What is the basic approach to tactical and strategic planning?

2. Is it more likely that the company will grow by acquisition, penetration of new markets, or increased market share?

3. To what extent are documented objectives used in planning?

4. Where is the emphasis placed for the development of new products (e.g., product-line extensions, new applications, new-product ventures, etc.)?

5. What are the plans for global or international growth?

6. What significant new products are under development?

Other Functional Areas

1. What is the background of the research and development manager?

2. What is the overall caliber of the research staff?

3. What is the company's technical position?

4. Does the company have idle plants and excess capacity?

5. What is the major research and development thrust?

6. How is research and development organized?

7. Is manufacturing productivity increasing or decreasing?

Market Analysis

Market analysis refers to studying the current and potential customers for a product or product line and then putting them into categories or segments. The segments are groups of customers with common demographics, common needs, and/or common uses for the product. The process of segmenting allows the marketer to get closer to the customer by focusing on the requirements of smaller groups.

It's important to break a total market into submarkets for a variety of reasons. First, it helps provide a better understanding of the aggregate market, including how and why customers buy. Second, it ensures better allocation of resources because the benefits that specific groups are looking for are better understood. This should make it possible to build competitive edges into the product. And, finally, segmentation enables the company to exploit opportunities by uncovering hidden niches.

To begin a market analysis, use segmentation factors most appropriate for the industry. (See Figure 5.2.) Consumer product companies use demographic variables such as age, family status, or lifestyle. Industrial product companies use the North American Industry Classification System (NAICS), company size, or functional titles. Service companies use intensity of need, risk categories, or distance from the company. Many companies use end-use of the product as a segmentation variable. For example, a product manager for nylon might break segments into end-use groups such as menswear, tires, and upholstery.

Komatsu's Long-Term Marketing Challenge

Komatsu, a Japanese manufacturer of bulldozers, developed a strategic vision of being a global player in earthmoving equipment, in essence a vision of beating Caterpillar. This required a series of short-term plans that focused on the immediate problems and opportunities Komatsu had to respond to in the process of achieving its long-term goal.

In the 1960s, Komatsu was about a third the size of Caterpillar, limited to one product line (small bulldozers), and scarcely represented outside of Japan. When Caterpillar threatened Komatsu in Japan, Komatsu's short-term objective was to protect its home market. The strategies used to accomplish this were product improvements, cost reductions, and new-product development through licensing agreements. In the early 1970s, Komatsu's challenge was to develop export markets. Since it was not yet strong enough to compete head-to-head with Caterpillar, it chose markets where Caterpillar was weak. Then, in the late 1970s Komatsu felt prepared to compete against Caterpillar in the U.S. market.

Note how the company started with a long-term vision or direction. Then, on a shorter-term basis it focused on the problems and

Komuatsu's Short-Term Challenges and Responses

Date	Corporate Challenge	Activities
Early 1960s	• Protect Komatsu's home market against Caterpillar	• Licensing deals with Cummins Engine, International Harvester, and Bucyrus-Eric
Mid-1960s	• Begin quality improvement efforts	• Several quality and cost-reduction programs
1960s to early 1970s	• Build export markets	• Komatsu Europe established • Service departments to assist newly industrializing countries
Late 1970s	• Create new products and markets	• Future and Frontiers program to identify new businesses based on society's needs and company's know-how

---

Komatsu's Long-Term Marketing Challenge (continued)

opportunities present at that time (i.e., "Where are we now?"). The corporate challenges represented the synthesis or "Where do we want to go" portion of the marketing planning process. In other words, they focused on the steps that needed to be taken at the current point in time to move closer to the future picture of the company. Finally, the activities column listed a brief summary of the action program or the tactics necessary to address the corporate challenges (i.e., "How are we going to get there?").

Source: Adapted from Gary Hamel and C. K. Prahalad, "Strategic Intent," *Harvard Business Review* (May–June 1989), 63–76.

After identifying segments that have different needs, examine the product's performance in each segment. What is the average order size, the share of segment sales, and the revenue generated? The example in Figure 5.3 shows four identifiable market segments. Segment A consists of the largest companies with special demands and the market power to negotiate for those demands. In rating the importance of six purchase criteria on a scale of 1 to 5 with 1 being "low importance" and 5 being "essential," price has an importance level of 4, quality/features is rated 1, delivery 3, installation 1, manufacturing/engineering support 1, and sales coverage 2. Based on industry data, the company estimates the overall sales in the segment are $89 million with an industry-average order size of $15,000. Its share of this market is 13 percent, with an average order size of $1,500. By studying all of the information, it appears that the company is most successful with Segments B and C. In both situations, there is a significant market share and the order size is greater than the industry average.[2]

After listing potential ways of segmenting the market, including both old and new market segments, the next step is to reduce the number of categories into a manageable number (3–7). First, eliminate any

Type of Factor	Product-Market	
	Consumer	**Business-to-Business**
Demographic	Age, sex, race	Industry (SIC or NAICS)
	Income	Geographic location
	Family size	Company size
	Family life-cycle	Functional decision
	stage	maker
	Location	Profitability
	Lifestyle	Risk categories
Application/use of product	Frequency of purchase	Application
	Size of purchase	Importance of purchase
	How product is used	Volume
		Frequency of purchase
Benefits (possibly beyond the product itself)	Desired benefits of product	Performance
	Psychological benefits	requirements
	Service	Support service
	Intensity of need	Desired features
		Service requirements

Figure 5.2 Segmentation Factors

segments that the firm cannot serve, for whatever reason. Then examine the remaining segments in terms of fit with company resources, fit with long-term strategy, cost to reach, and risk to serve. Rank these segments so that the greatest proportion of resources will be devoted to the most important segments and the lowest proportion of resources to the least important segments. Chapter 6 details the process of market segmentation and customer value management.

Competitive Analysis

The competitive analysis is a summary of what might be pages (or even files) of information compiled from published and internal sources. Annual reports, newspaper articles, trade shows, salespeople, government and trade association reports, and informal conver-

Common purchase-decision criteria	Segment A	Segment B	Segment C	Segment D
	• "Category killers" • Standard products • Large purchases • Strong price negotiators	• Large customers • Very price-sensitive • Standard products • Large purchases	• Medium-size customers • Modified standard products • Medium-size lots • Fairly price-sensitive	• Any-size customer • Nonstandard motors • Small lots • Price often secondary
Price	• • • •	• • •	• •	•
Quality/features	•	• •	• • •	• • • •
Delivery	• • •	• •	• •	• •
Installation	•	•	• •	• •
Marketing/ engineering support	•	• •	• • • •	• • • • •
Sales coverage	• •	• •	• • •	• • • • •
Size and share	$89 million 13%	$113.4 million 31%	$69.3 million 30%	$66.6 million 25%
Average order size	$1,500 Industry: $15,000	$6,998 Industry: $5,000	$2,345 Industry: $2,000	$923 Industry: $1,100

Key to importance of buying factors:

1	2	3	4	5
•	• •	• • •	• • • •	• • • • •
Least important				Most important

Figure 5.3 Segmentation by Key Buying Factors

sations with customers can provide much of the necessary information. However, to analyze customer perceptions of the competitive strengths and weaknesses, some type of marketing research is necessary. (See Worksheet 5.2.)

Competitive intelligence is an important part of a product manager's job. Part of the responsibility is to understand a product's competition so that threats can be minimized. Start with the most easily obtained data, including published information. Financial reports, pub-

General Information for Fy___

Division: **Group:**   **Product Line:**   **Market:**

	Your Product	Product A	Product B	Product C	Product D
Sales volume (units)					
Sales revenues ($)					
Profit					
Market share					
Target market(s)					
General product strategy					
Product differentiation					
Customer image					
General price strategy					
Average/list price					
General promotion strategy					
General distribution strategy					
Sales force size					
Sales force strengths					

Worksheet 5.2 Competitive Analysis

lished price lists, competitive ads and promotional materials, product spec sheets, and trade articles can provide a wealth of information if analyzed. The financial reports can provide clues about future strategies; the ads can suggest how the competitor is positioning the product; and the specification sheets can help in benchmarking.

If the competition is a privately held company or a division of a larger company, subscribe to the local newspaper where the product is manufactured. Or subscribe to an on-line search service to monitor the main competitor.

In analyzing information, do not stop with the current, static data. Look at the data over time to study trends and changes that might help develop assumptions about competitive marketing strategies. Identifying possible competitive marketing strategies provides the information necessary to predict future actions or reactions to tactical maneuvers.

Competitors and Competing Products

Maintaining your product's competitive edge requires a continuous updating of competitor intelligence. For specific tips on gathering this type of information contact the Society of Competitive Intelligence Professionals at www.scip.org.

1. To which competitors have you lost business and from which have you gained business? (This is the competition from the customer's perspective.)

2. Where (in what regions, applications, industries, etc.) is competition the strongest? Why?

3. What are the corporate competencies of the companies that own competing products? What is the relationship between the competencies and the products?

4. What are the list prices of the competing products? The actual prices?

5. What is the market perception of the competing products? Awareness level? Customer loyalty?

6. Are there any specific product features that are "best-in-class," against which your product should be benchmarked?

7. Is the competing product a small percentage of its company's business, or is it the main product of the company? How important are the sales to the competitor, and how much is the company willing to invest to protect these sales?

Division:　　**Group:**　　　**Product Line:**　　**Market:**

	20___ Plan	20___ Actual	20___ Plan	20___ Actual	20___ Plan	20___ Actual
Industry volume (units)						
Your volume						
Percentage of industry volume						
Industry sales ($)						
Your sales						
Percentage of industry sales						
Product sales as percentage of company sales						
Cost of goods sold						
Gross margin						
Gross margin ratio						
Controllable costs						
Promotion						
Field sales costs						
Other marketing costs						
Misc. controllable costs						
Total controllable costs						
Net profit contribution						
Quality index						
New product sales						
Target account sales						
Price index						
Sales per salesperson						
Product/line strengths						
Product/line weaknesses						

Worksheet 5.3 Performance History

Performance History

The performance history looks at how well a product performed over time and relative to plan. It focuses attention on the market share and financial and other numeric or statistical indicators of performance. In addition, answers to product mix questions like the ones listed below provide qualitative data that could highlight problems and opportunities to be addressed in the marketing plan. (See Worksheet 5.3.)

Existing Customers

Although most of these questions were raised during the market analysis, revisiting them helps avoid overlooking opportunities or challenges that need to be addressed:

1. Is there a group of heavy users of the product(s)? What percentage of the purchasers do they constitute?

2. Is the primary target market growing, stable, or declining?

3. Under what circumstances do customers purchase the product(s)?

4. How and why is geographical coverage limited?

5. What percentage of customers are national accounts? International?

6. Are most customers new or repeat buyers?

7. Are the customers the end-users? If not, what information is available about the end-user?

8. Are your customers progressive? Traditional? Passive?

9. How sensitive have customers been to past price changes?

10. Does the customer base consist of a few large customers or many small buyers?

The Product

Data on the sales and profitability of the product is most likely routinely provided by your accounting department, but the analysis should go beyond quantitative statistics to include qualitative variables:

1. What does the name of the product imply? Can it be branded?

2. Which of the features are distinguishable by the customer?

3. For each feature, ask "So what?" to identify the benefits from the customer's point of view.

4. Is the product supplied through intermediaries (e.g., dealers)? If so, the analysis of features/benefits should be handled in two steps.

5. If a numeric rating were given to the product quality (with 1 being low and 7 being high), what would that rating be? Would the rating be the same from the customers?

6. What does each item in the product line contribute to sales and profits? To customer satisfaction? Can some of the products be pruned?

7. How does the product line rate of return compare with the company's overall rate of return?

8. Is the product design conducive to an efficient manufacturing process?

9. What are the engineering costs for product development, product engineering, and manufacturing engineering?

10. What is the unit break-even sales for the product?

11. Are product guarantees competitive?

12. What would happen if the products were more standardized? More customized?

13. What is the company's attitude toward private labeling?

The Sales Force

Even though product managers typically have no authority over the salespeople, an examination of sales force effectiveness can highlight potential opportunities or problems that need to be addressed in the marketing plan:

1. Is the current sales force structure appropriate for achieving the product objectives?

2. Are the target customers being reached in the most effective manner?

3. How effective has the product/sales training been?

4. What sales tools do the salespeople actually use to sell the product?

5. Has the sales force been taught how to help customers visualize the benefits of the product?

Pricing

The "right" price covers all relevant costs, is positioned appropriately given the competitive value of the products, and takes into account customer perceptions. The product manager should assess whether company policies enable that to happen.

1. Have significant amounts of business been lost because of product prices?

2. Are errors frequently made in pricing?

3. What is the perceived cost of buying the product/service?

4. Is the company a price leader or a price follower?

5. What is the pricing policy of the company?

6. What types of discounts are offered? How does that compare with the competition?

The Promotional Campaigns

Promotional campaigns should be part of an integrated marketing communications effort, with the product manager pushing for a consistent message to customers.

1. What is the current image customers have of the product? Is it consistent with the advertising?

2. Did prior advertising strategies work? Why or why not?

3. What nonadvertising promotion has been tried? How well did it work?

The Distribution Strategy

The sales force and distributors may be the most important face-to-face contacts with customers. The effectiveness of these contacts cannot be left to chance and should be built into the marketing plan.

1. What is the company's relationship with intermediaries (e.g., distributors, agents, retailers, etc.)?

2. What are the channels of distribution? What percentage of the product sales are through each type of intermediary?

3. What are distribution costs as a percentage of sales?

4. How does the company's policy for distributor/retailer margins compare with those of the competition?

5. What has been the recent history of stock-outs, substitutes, and back orders?

Support Services

To complete the full cycle of customer value, installation and repair services should be considered in the marketing plan.

1. Has the value of repair services changed (due to cost increases, repair person efficiency, or any other reason)?

Trend Dynamics

An examination of trends and their dynamics relative to a product's success is the final part of the background analysis. External trends have a direct bearing on market potential even though they are a less tangible part of the analysis. In answering the following questions, select major events that are likely to affect the company, the competitors, the product, and markets served by the company:

1. What technological changes are likely? How might they impact product sales within the next several years?

2. What have been the industry trends in the following areas:

- Product changes
- Price levels/policies
- Distribution changes
- Mergers/acquisitions/divestitures
- Power shifts in the channel

3. What leading indicators correspond with product sales?

4. What are the basic trends and changes in the economy?

5. Are there regulatory or political forces that could impact product sales? What are their trends?

6. What is the probability of the above trends occurring?

7. What impact do these have on the product(s)?

Checklist: The Product Marketing Planning Process

✓ Start the annual planning process by carefully assessing the current status of your product and your company. Look for problems to address during the next fiscal year as well as opportunities to exploit.

✓ Assign your customers to groups or segments that allow you to allocate your resources most effectively and provide you the greatest competitive opportunities. Don't be afraid to think about your customers in new ways.

✓ Begin your competitive analysis by asking yourself to whom have you lost the most business or from whom have you gained the most business. Don't limit your analysis to only the top companies in the industry.

✓ Study the performance of your product(s) over a three-year period. Look at the stability of the customers for each product, the effectiveness of prices and price changes, the sales and profit trends by product, the attitude of the sales force, and any other variables that could explain differences in performance.

✓ Try to predict the effect current trends will have on the future of your product. Are regulatory forces likely to require design changes? Are there indications customers are shifting in preference toward competing technologies? Whenever possible, prepare for the potential changes before you are forced to.

6

Customer Value Management

As EXPLAINED IN Chapter 5, the cornerstone of an effective business strategy is the ability to attract and retain high-profit customers. There should be more focus on growing customers than on just growing product sales. Consequently, product managers must have a clear-cut understanding and appreciation of the market(s) for their products. These markets could include existing customers as well as potential customers, singular clients as well as groups or segments, and individuals *using* your product as well as those *influencing* its purchase. This chapter focuses on the issues involved in analyzing your markets and establishing plans to maximize their profitability.

The starting point for most product managers is to simultaneously evaluate the attractiveness of different markets and determine their firm's ability to satisfy the needs of those markets. All customers are not created equal, and trying to build loyalty among all customers can be detrimental to the health of a firm. Product managers must determine which customers offer the best future return on investment. For mass-market products (e.g., fast-moving consumer goods—FMCG), profiling heavy users and developing a plan to appeal to them is common. The profile might include standard demographic variables such as age, sex, income, geographic location, marital status, and family size, as well as psychographic characteristics such as perceptions of oneself and desired personality characteristics. For industrial products (e.g., capital equipment), customers requiring specific applications or uses may be more profitable than others and therefore considered the "best" customers. After defining the best customers, the next step is to attract more like them and/or enhance the profitability of the existing customers. The flow chart of customer analysis is featured in Figure 6.1.

Customer Analysis Process

Let's use an example of a hypothetical food service company called Progressive Foodservice, Inc., that sells food items to two major market categories: food service distributors and operators, each of which may be further segmented. The food service distributors consist of full-line distributors, specialty distributors, and buying groups. The food service operators consist of commercial operators (lodging, fast-food, restaurants, cafeterias, caterers, and retail hosts) and noncommercial operators (health care, educational institutions, airlines, and vending). Starting at the highest level of segmentation, the first step is to determine what needs are distinctly different among the segments. Assume that the full-service distributors and distributor buying groups are interested in centralized purchasing, volume buying to get a discounted price, and specialized distribution specifications. The specialty distributors, who carry a specific line of products or target a specific type of account, are interested in unique products and possible merchandising support to reach their customers.

For those sales directly to food service operators rather than through distributors, customers also have varying needs. Within the commercial group, fast-food restaurants demand just-in-time shipments of food products at the lowest possible price. The remaining commercial operators (to varying degrees) desire menu support and presentation ideas. The noncommercial operators are interested in consistent inventory replenishment and long shelf-life products. After studying these needs, Progressive recombined the markets into five broad need segments then looked at two things: (1) how attractive the segments are as a whole and (2) whether the firm had any competitive advantages in addressing the segment needs.

To determine market attractiveness, Progressive examined market size (the total number of customers in each segment), the growth rate, the strength of competition, the price sensitivity of the customers, the

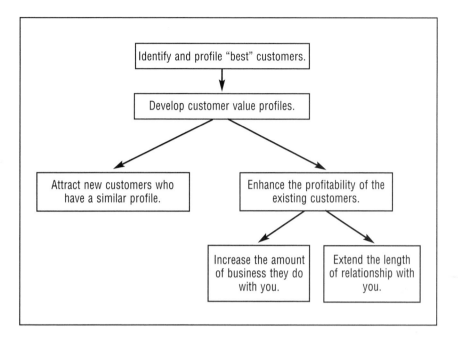

Figure 6.1 Flow Chart of Customer Analysis Process

revenue and profitability of existing customers in these segments, and similar variables. Then it rated each segment on a 1–5 scale with 1 being "unattractive" and 5 being "highly attractive." General distributors (segment A) were rated 3, specialty distributors (segment B) were rated 4, fast-food chains (segment C) were rated 2, commercial operators (segment D) were rated 3, and noncommercial operators (segment E) were rated 1. Note that there is some blurring of customers and non-customers at this time, since we don't want to limit the analysis to what is happening now but keep in mind the potential for growth. Compare the size, purchase volumes, and growth rate for each segment in the entire market with the size, purchase volumes, and growth rate for the respective segment of existing customers. Ask questions during this analysis. What is the demand in each segment for the product? What is the product's penetration? How many prospects are there in segments that purchase only competitive products? Why do they purchase only those products? Are you gaining or losing share? Do you participate in the most profitable segments in the industry? Summarize the information in a table similar to that shown in Figure 6.2.

Market Segment	Percentage of Company Sales	Percentage of Industry Sales	Characteristics of Market Attractiveness (size, growth rate, purchase volumes, etc.)	Rating (1–5)
General distributors	39%	27%	Top five play a pivotal role in the industry. Price is a driving factor.	3
Specialty distributors	14%	13%	Showing growth due to special food service demands of aging population.	4
Fast-food chains	16%	22%	Approaching saturation for our type of product. Heavy competition and price pressure.	2
Commercial operators	22%	30%	Pockets of rapid growth (e.g., retail delis) due to dual-income families. Strong potential for our type of product.	3
Noncommercial operators	9%	8%	Static or declining potential.	1

Figure 6.2 Attractiveness Ratings of Market Segments for Progressive Foodservice, Inc.

To determine whether it had any competitive advantages in addressing the segment-specific needs, Progressive honestly appraised its own competencies and rated its ability to satisfy the needs of the segments. Again using a 1–5 scale, Progressive rated itself 1 if there were strong competitors with significant abilities to satisfy the specific needs, 3 if it was at the same level as the competition, and 5 if it was significantly superior to the competition. Progressive's competitive ability-to-serve ratings are shown in Figure 6.3. The "Requirements to Satisfy Needs" column highlights improvements or changes Progressive would need to make to address the needs of each of the five identified segments. The ratings identify how well Progressive can meet the needs compared to its competitors.

Combining the information on market attractiveness and ability to serve yields the matrix shown in Figure 6.4. For example, the General distributors segment has a "3" for market attractiveness and a "3" for ability to satisfy needs, placing it right in the center.

All else being equal, the best target market(s) would be in the upper right-hand quadrant where a company has determined it has a highly

Market Segment	Needs	Requirements to Satisfy Needs *(products, skill set, locations, costs)*	Rating *(1–5)*
General distributors	Centralized purchasing; volume buying at discounted price; specialized distribution specifications	Improved carrier terms, established extranet	3
Specialty distributors	Unique products; merchandising support	Commitment to R & D and new product development	4
Fast-food chains	Just-in-time shipments at lowest possible price	Shared cost shipping services	2
Commercial operators	Menu support; presentation suggestions	Consulting *chef de cuisine* on call; test kitchens; educational CD-ROMs	4
Noncommercial operators	Consistent inventory replenishment; long shelf-life products	Product development efforts on extending shelf life	1

Figure 6.3 Ability-to-Serve Ratings for Progressive Foodservice, Inc.

attractive customer segment and a high competitive advantage in serving the segment. As expected, there are other considerations. First, there may be no segment that falls solidly in this quadrant. In that case, a firm might target the most attractive segment that exists and determine what products and skills it would be necessary to develop to shift the segment to the right. Second, there may be a segment in the upper right quadrant having relatively little *future* profit potential compared with other segments. To help visualize this, the circles can be adjusted in size to represent the potential opportunity in that segment. Third, a segment in the upper right quadrant could already be dominated by the company, with little to be gained by increased resources. In that case, allocating sufficient marketing dollars to customer retention may be appropriate, with more resources being diverted to other promising segments. To help visualize this in the matrix, it is useful to draw the circles as pie charts with a distinction between attained market and future potential. Finally, some segments that appear to be less attractive on an *absolute* basis might indeed turn out to be quite attractive if they are underserved by the competition.

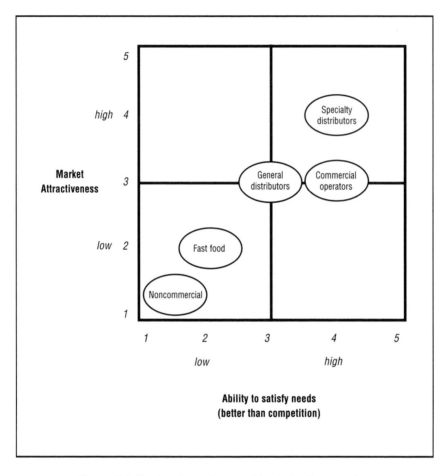

Figure 6.4 Market Attractiveness Matrix for Progressive
Foodservice, Inc.

To compile this information, both internal and secondary (published) sources are necessary. From an internal perspective, sales records should be correlated with demographic characteristics to determine which variables relate most closely to profitability. Does company size, geographic location, type of application, or any other variable help "predict" sales? Once these variables are identified, you can extrapolate them to noncustomers to estimate market and growth potentials. The "deliverable" from this step of the background analysis is a "knowledge chapter" in the product fact book summarizing the drivers of loyalty and defining profitable customer segments.

Market Segment	Percentage of Company Sales	Percentage of Industry Sales	Characteristics of Market Attractiveness (size, growth rate, purchase volumes, etc.)	Rating (1–5)
Segment A				
Segment B				
Segment C				
Segment D				
Segment E				

Worksheet 6.1 Attractiveness Ratings of Market Segments

It's worth noting that as companies design and implement new services to satisfy customer expectations, their processes usually become more complex and costs usually increase. Conventional cost-accounting methods do not properly identify differences in cost-to-serve. They fail to identify some of the postproduction costs that are caused by addressing segment-specific needs. As will be discussed in Chapter 11, it's important to recognize that costs are not just uncontrollable occurrences, but rather are caused by measurable factors that can be managed. Therefore, an understanding of segment reporting and possibly activity-based costing needs to be part of the product manager's repertoire of skills.

Market Segment	Needs	Requirements to Satisfy Needs (products, skill set, locations, costs)	Rating (1–5)
Segment A			
Segment B			
Segment C			
Segment D			
Segment E			

Worksheet 6.2 Ability-to-Serve Ratings by Market Segment

Once these two worksheets are completed, the product manager can create the visual matrix described earlier for Progressive Foodservice, Inc. The information can then be used to identify primary and secondary target markets, their needs, and the issues a firm will need to address to satisfy the needs.

Balancing Customer Retention and Customer Acquisition

Once the profiling of the target market is completed, the next question is how to *grow* customer equity. This could involve one or a combina-

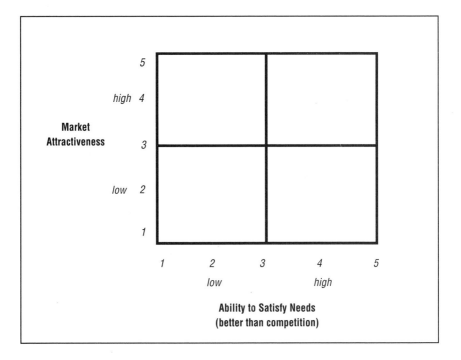

Worksheet 6.3 Market Attractiveness Matrix

tion of (a) increasing the profitability of existing customers, (b) attracting new customers with the potential for future high-value business, or (c) "firing" low-potential customers. To increase existing profitability, invest in the highest-value customers first. How can add-on sales and cross-selling (of even other product managers' products!) increase customer equity? (Don't let a product or brand management focus hurt this effort. Remember that brands don't create wealth; customers do.) What behaviors do you want to change in the market to increase its profitability? What behaviors do you need to change in your own company to increase profitability?

Database programs can help product managers understand the specific needs of segments and subsegments. (See Chapter 4 for a discussion of customer relationship management software.) Product managers should try to determine what activities would be necessary to get existing customers to increase the amount of business they do with the firm, to get "good" customers to become more loyal, and to get secondary customers converted into primary customers. Then, by taking advantage of flexible manufacturing and delivery, they can provide cost-effective offerings tailored to each group—offerings such as product features, price discounts, service arrangements, and purchase warranties. This approach has been used by industrial firms, by service-sector companies, and by resellers such as wholesalers and retailers. A Canadian grocery store chain, for example, analyzed a "typical" store with around 15,000 households, annual revenues of $25 million and an operating margin of 2 percent.

> First, the company segmented the customer base surrounding the store into three categories: primary shoppers (those who give the store 80 percent or more of their grocery business), secondary shoppers (those who spend more than 10 percent but less than 50 percent of their grocery budget at the store), and nonshoppers.
>
> Second, the company calculated the impact on the store's profitability of small improvements in the behavior profiles of existing customers. Given the fixed cost structure of a grocery store, the contribution margin from each additional dollar spent by a customer can earn ten times the store's net profit margin. Thus, the company found that even small improvements in one of many customer behaviors led to very significant profitability gains. Expanding the customer base by 2 percent with primary shoppers, for example, would increase the store's profitability by more than 45 percent. Converting just two hundred secondary customers into primary customers would increase profitability by more than 20 percent. Selling one more produce item to every customer would increase profitability by more than 40 percent. Persuading every customer to substitute two store-brand items for two national-brand items each time they visited the store would increase profitability by 55 percent. . . .
>
> Rather than focusing directly on these opportunities, though, the company, like most other organizations, had been paying attention to more traditional objectives, such as productivity, market share, and quality. As a result, it had overlooked the possibility of closing this full-potential gap by optimizing customer value exchanges.[1]

Firing Your Customers

A particular challenge many product managers face is saying "no" to an unprofitable customer. All companies have customers who demand special services (with no additional revenue generated), who demand "rock-bottom" prices for everything, or who require changing the basic product or service to fit their unique needs. When this is the case, there

Customer Loyalty in a Commodity World

Can traditional concepts like market segmentation and niche marketing work in the new millennium? Can there be loyal customers when the Internet opens up the ability for customers to pick and choose products and services based on price? Every indication suggests there *are* still opportunities to uncover and satisfy customer needs using electronic tools as an ally rather than as the enemy. This requires getting solid information from customers and cementing relationships with them. Some companies are using "permission marketing" to get customers to willingly supply data that aids in marketing decisions.

> This . . . is happening right now between American Isuzu Motors Inc., and its on-line partners. Isuzu's customers and prospects receive a mailer directing them to visit Isuzu's site to create their favorite vehicle on-line, get a dealer quote, and tell Isuzu when they are planning to purchase their next vehicle. In exchange, the car shopper receives a $10 gift certificate good for purchases from on-line retailers CD now, CBS Sportsline, and GreatFood.com. American Isuzu Motors gets powerful information, including customer preferences such as type of vehicle, trim level, color, model, and, most importantly, when the customer is planning to purchase a vehicle and from what dealer. Then, armed with this data, American Isuzu Motors can deliver enhanced offers to those customers who have indicated certain preferences and timing.

Yahoo has also obtained data on customers that allows personalized features for individual members. It has created "stickiness" in its site and is careful not to spam all of its registrants, sending only E-mail messages of interest.

> A woman in Peoria, Illinois, pulls up Yahoo, checks the news and stock quotes bookmarked on her *My Yahoo* home page, and reviews E-mail in her account at yahoo.com. She's thirty today. Look: an E-card from Yahoo's Birthday Club—and $50 off at her favorite on-line store. Now that she's so much older and wiser, she decides to look for a bigger apartment in the Yahoo classifieds. And since she deserves a treat today, she bids on vintage pearl earrings in Yahoo's auction area.

Customer Loyalty in a Commodity World (continued)

The Internet is not the only way to increase loyalty and improve segmentation effectiveness. Better policies for the sales force can also help. You might consider paying lower commissions for "price" buyers or former customers (who have proved they are not loyal) and offer higher rewards to acquiring customers who tend to be loyal and to buy multiple products. That means you have to determine the characteristics of customers who are more valuable to the firm and pay salespeople for obtaining new customers with these characteristics. Xerox has established a program to link customer value to the compensation of the sales force and to use them as a tool in customer-relationship management.

Source: Condensed from Don Peppers and Martha Rogers, "The Price of Customer Service," *Sales and Marketing Management* (April 1999): 20–21; Eryn Brown, et. al., "9 Ways to Win on the Web," *Fortune* (May 24, 1999): 112–125; and Robert McKim, "Information: The Newest Currency," *Target Marketing* (July 1999): 36–37+.

---

are only a few options available: raise the price, reduce the cost of servicing the customer, or discontinue doing business with the customer.

Raising the price to compensate for the value being supplied is the most obvious solution. However, this may be difficult at best. The customer must perceive and believe in the competitive value, and if the customer is not part of the target market there may not be a good "fit" between their needs and your firm's capabilities. That leads to the second option: reducing the cost to serve. It's crucial that the product manager clearly understand the total costs "caused by" the customer (see Chapter 11 on contribution reporting). Only by understanding the true costs can an effort be made to reduce them.

Discontinuing business with a customer may be a last but necessary resort. Typically it happens indirectly through the changing of policies or raising of prices. However, before this happens, ask a few questions. Does this customer bring in business simply by being a customer? Will this customer grow into a strategic customer in the future? Does the customer absorb overhead that would need to be allocated elsewhere if the business relationship is ended? Provide an honest appraisal of the situation, and be prepared to say "no" if necessary.

Checklist: Customer Value Management

✓ In profiling "good" customers, consider factors such as profitability, market size and growth rate, reference value for other customers, and level of price sensitivity.

✓ Evaluate your ability to satisfy customer needs better than the competition.

✓ Combine market attractiveness and ability-to-serve evaluations to prioritize market segments and customers.

✓ Have a balance between customer acquisition and customer retention.

✓ In developing strategies, decide what you want various customer segments to *do* as a result of your marketing efforts.

✓ Practice the art of saying "no" by designing policies and products specifically for targeted customers.

7

The Annual Product Plan

CHAPTERS 5 AND 6 described the background analysis, with a special emphasis on understanding customers and prospects, as the prelude for developing the marketing plan. Armed with this information, product managers are able to set visions or targets for their products. However, a target without a plan is just a dream. So this chapter discusses the process of turning dreams into plans.

Synthesis: Where Do You Want to Go?

The synthesis is the section of the annual product marketing plan that ties together the background analysis with the vision by indicating what steps will be taken this fiscal year to move closer to the future picture of the company's product line. It starts with the identification of problems and opportunities that need to be addressed in the annual plan. Then it moves to the forecast of sales volume, the marketing objectives that specify the market segments from which the volume will be generated, and the positioning of the product in the customers' minds.

Problems and Opportunities

After examining the market, the competition, the historical performance, and any significant trends, the next step is to synthesize the information to look for problems or opportunities and decide where to go from there. Problems or opportunities are the conclusions drawn from any part of the background analysis. For example, the analysis might uncover new niches that previously had been overlooked, a declining market share that was camouflaged by a growing market segment, or an inconsistent product image. In any case, focus on problems to correct or opportunities to leverage in the product marketing plan. Without this step of drawing conclusions, the background analysis is often perceived as a waste of time and is not made relevant to the marketing plan.

Setting marketing and sales objectives follows the identification of problems and opportunities. Frequently a product manager is given a financial sales goal, and his or her job is to design a marketing program to make it happen. In other cases, the product manager must present the sales forecast to management with a justification or rationale. Typically, there is some combination of the two approaches.

Sales Forecasting

The product manager is responsible for forecasting product sales or, at a minimum, understanding the forecasts received. There are three categories of forecasting techniques that might be used:

1. **Time series forecasts** can be obtained from historical data on past product sales to project into the future for short-term sales figures.

2. **Compiled forecasts**, as the term implies, are compilations of data from qualitative and quantitative research.

3. **Causal forecasts** are derived from relating sales to the factors that cause the sales to happen.

Although a product manager usually works with an analyst to obtain these figures, it is important to understand the basic ramifications of the three categories of forecasts.

Time Series A logical place to start forecasting future sales is to look at historical sales patterns. Time series analyses look at changes in sales over time. Plotting a product's sales over time gives the product manager a picture of the product's sales trends. Trend-fitting, or regression,

Hewlett-Packard: Problems and Opportunities for the Deskjet

Hewlett-Packard introduced the Deskjet in 1988. Sales came slowly. By 1989, the product wasn't meeting its sales goals, even though there was an absence of strong competition. An analysis determined that the Deskjet was taking business away from H-P's own laser printers, rather than the competition, resulting in a lower profit margin per sale.

After identifying the problem, H-P decided to reposition the Deskjet as a competitor to dot-matrix printers instead of as a lower-cost alternative to laser printers. To attain this objective, H-P started by thoroughly studying Epson, the leader in the industry. The company began to track Epson's market share. It evaluated Epson's marketing practices, profiled its top managers, and surveyed its customers. Engineers tore apart Epson printers to better understand the technology used. H-P discovered that Epson printers were placed in prominent spots in stores, customers perceived the printers as reliable, and the products were designed for easy manufacturability.

Armed with this information, Hewlett-Packard planned the actions that were necessary to reposition the Deskjet. First, the company convinced stores to place Deskjets next to the Epson dot-matrix printers to emphasize the competitive positioning. Second, H-P extended its warranty to three years to assure buyers that the Deskjet was reliable. And finally, the inkjets were redesigned with manufacturability in mind.

Source: Adapted from Stephen Kreider Yoder, "How H-P Used Tactics of the Japanese to Beat Them at Their Game," *Wall Street Journal* (September 8, 1994): 1+.

plots the sales over time and uses a statistical formula to fit a line through the data points and then project that line into the future. Trend-fitting is relatively simple and fast to do by computer and is easy to understand. It can be accurate in the short term if there are no external factors that make the future sales environment significantly different from the past sales environment.

There are several averages that are time-series based. A moving average forecasts sales using a given number of time periods from the past (e.g., the average of the past twelve months' data). Each data point has the same weight unless seasonal indexes or other weights are built in. As the average moves into the future, it drops off the oldest data point from the calculations. Exponential smoothing is a form of moving average that provides heavier weights to the most recent data. This is done because it is assumed that recent data are more valuable in predicting future sales than older data.

Box-Jenkins is a more sophisticated version of exponential smoothing. This technique uses a computer to test different time series models for the best fit. For example, the number of data points as well as the different weights affect the time-series line, so it is important to track how effective the various techniques were in providing a mathematical line close to the actual line of sales points.

Time-series techniques are appropriate when the sales environment does not change and when the effectiveness of a marketing plan has no impact on sales. Generally, neither of these is true. As a result, marketing research information and/or causal information should be part of the forecasting process.

Compiled Forecasts The marketing research approach used for forecasting can be a combination of compiling secondary and primary data as well as qualitative and quantitative approaches to data collection. Some of the secondary data can be pulled from the product fact book. Worksheet 5.3 in Chapter 5 provides information on industry/category sales for a product/line. Look at average market share over time and multiply this average by the projected industry sales for the next fiscal year. The result is an approximate sales forecast based on the industry projection. Adjust this forecast using qualitative information on trends or other elements that could influence product sales.

In terms of primary data collection, both qualitative and quantitative inputs are important. Quantitative input can come from front-line sources. Salespeople provide estimates by account or territory and regional managers provide estimates by distributor or channel type. An example sales force customer analysis form is shown in Figure 7.1. In the example, the salespeople are asked to estimate sales for each major account for selected products, with their best estimate of the

Account	Product A		Product B		Product C	
	Sales	Probability	Sales	Probability	Sales	Probability
Vaporware	$1,000	.60	$600	.60	$400	.60
Tunnel Vision	2,000	.50	700	.80	700	.60
Virus-Aid	1,500	.70	900	.75	300	.90
Data-Notes	1,000	.50	600	.96	600	.80

Figure 7.1 Sales Force Customer Analysis Form

probability of closing the sale during the upcoming quarter. The form can be adapted to include volume rather than dollar revenue, annual rather than quarterly estimates, or other industry-specific variables. The product manager (or analyst) can calculate the expected values by multiplying the sales estimates for each product by the relevant probabilities. In the example, the expected sales of Product A for this particular salesperson would be $3,150 (the sum of the sales times the probability for each account). Customers can also be surveyed directly to assess their probable purchases by product or for the entire line.

Qualitative forecasting techniques are also useful, particularly for new products. Concept testing, in conjunction with intent-to-buy surveys, can be a data point for the new product forecast. Other tools include the Delphi technique and trade data.

Causal or Correlation-Based Forecasts Causal techniques attempt to find relationships between sales and other variables. For example, tire sales are related to vehicular sales, and sales of many household products are related to housing starts. If there are leading indicators (such as vehicle sales or housing starts) that can be used to better understand the sales environment for a product, they should be used in the forecasting process. Sales can also be affected by advertising expenditures, number of salespeople, price changes, or other marketing variables. If a causal relationship between a change in marketing expenditures and a change in sales can be demonstrated, that information can be used not only in forecasting, but also as justification for spending a given amount in the marketing plan.

The forecasted sales figures used in a marketing plan should be based on a variety of inputs. Do not rely exclusively on trend projections, and do not accept upper management's sales forecasts without question. Try to reconcile the unit and dollar amounts based on the background analysis and the anticipated marketing plan/budget.

Objectives and Strategies

The next step is to develop objectives and strategies. The objectives answer the question, "What do you want to happen?" or "What do you need to do to reach the sales forecast?" The strategy states the "how" of the objectives. The objectives should be stated in numeric format whenever possible so that they are measurable. Objectives can be in terms of units or dollars (revenue and/or margin), market share, customer satisfaction level, and so on. The objective starts with a verb (increase, maintain, solidify, etc.), acting on a specific goal (repeat purchases, new trial, sales volume/revenue, etc.) for a stated market (existing customers, new customers, or an identified market segment) within a specified time (during the last quarter, within the next twelve months, etc.). An example objective is as follows:

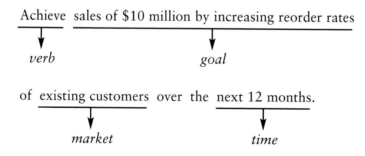

Justify the objectives by providing rationale from the customer analysis and other worksheets in previous chapters. For example, if the background analysis uncovered the fact that reorder rates are declining even though customer satisfaction is high and there are no obvious problems, it could be argued that the objective can be obtained if appropriate support is provided. Typically, there will be a general marketing objective, followed by specific objective and strategy statements for each element of the marketing mix (as appropriate for a firm). Always make sure that the entire plan is coordinated so that it has maximum effectiveness.

Positioning

The next part of the synthesis phase is positioning—deciding how a product is to be perceived in the minds of the customer, relative to the competition. Imagine talking to a customer who asks, "Why should I buy from you?" What should your answer be? What makes your product a better buy than competitive products? In this analysis, consider the customer's frame of reference (i.e., the products they would consider likely competitors). Different customers will have different frames of reference that would require different positionings. Therefore, the positioning statement should identify the relevant market segment, that segment's frame of reference, the product's point of differentiation, and an indication of why a product provides that differentiation (i.e., the internal strength of competitive edge that makes a claim of differentiation credible). A positioning statement might resemble the following:

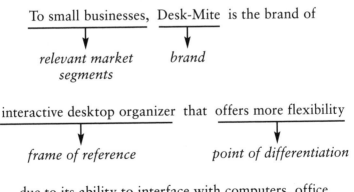

The Importance of Customer Retention as a Marketing Objective

Companies are realizing that customer retention is as, if not more, important than getting new customers. According to *Business Marketing* magazine:

> An October 1994 study by Marketing Metrics showed that of the 165 companies surveyed, respondents, on average, allocate 53 percent of marketing budgets to retain existing customers and 47 percent to win new customers. A similar 1991 study showed 46 percent of marketing budgets went to retention, while 54 percent went to acquiring new customers.

Cellular One of New York and New Jersey, for example, has part of its marketing department devoted solely to customer retention. Some of the tactics include a 24-hour Customer Care Center and a Corporate Care Center for special corporate accounts. David Straus, director of customer base marketing, says, "Our job really starts once the customer is in the door."

New York-based Bowne & Co., one of the world's largest financial printers, publishes a customer newsletter as a tool in customer retention. By keeping customers abreast of changes in their industries, Bowne & Co. is better able to differentiate itself from other financial service providers.

Source: Adapted from Kim Cleland, "Firms Want Customers Coming Back for More," *Business Marketing* (January 1995): 4+.

Start by identifying the attributes customers are looking for when they buy from the product category, and find out how important each attribute is. Is delivery important? How about minimum tolerances? How important? Next, have customers rate the product in question versus the competition along all the important attributes. Try to isolate attributes for which customers already believe the product is competitively superior and that the company can protect using its core abili-

Division: **Group:** **Product Line:** **Market:**

General marketing objective(s):

Rationale for objective(s):

Positioning statement:

To _____ ,

_____ is the brand of
(market segment)   (your product name)

_____ that

_____

Worksheet 7.1 Marketing Objectives and Strategies

ties, knowledge, or other strength. If this cannot be found, the job of
the product manager is to determine how to build it into the product.
(See Worksheet 7.1.)

The Action Program: How Are We Going to Get There?

The purpose of the annual product marketing plan is to provide top
management with a concise marketing and financial summary of objectives and strategies along with the requirements to achieve the objectives.
There should be enough rationale to allow them to approve the necessary expenditures without the detail available in a product fact book.
Keep the plan as brief as possible, perhaps no more than six or eight
pages (excluding charts and exhibits). Too much detail obscures the
main issues involved.

On the other hand, do not use the desire for brevity as an excuse
for not collecting information. If some information needed to support
a recommendation is not available, mention it in the plan (at least as a

footnote) to demonstrate that critical data are not being ignored, but that there is sufficient confidence with the other information to justify taking the risk.

If the product plan is to be presented orally as part of a meeting, be sure to come prepared to answer any questions that might arise. Nothing is more frustrating to top management than to reschedule a meeting or make it longer than necessary because of a product manager's lack of preparation.

The written plan consists of a summary of the product's historical performance, a statement of problems and opportunities, sales forecasts/goals and a summary table of the impact on profit and loss (P & L), marketing objectives for the product or product line, concise strategies for accomplishing the objectives, and a series of financial and other exhibits to permit a quick assessment of the product program and its impact.

Separate strategy documents might need to be prepared for operational use by the product manager. Simply provide a concise summary of each as part of the annual product plan, perhaps in the format of listing the objective(s) for that element of the program and providing a brief overview of the strategy to accomplish that objective. Be careful, however, that the complete plan is coordinated. Do not work on the advertising strategy document, for example, without coordinating it with the other elements of the marketing mix.

There are several possible formats for a written product plan; there is no one best approach. Figure 7.2 is only an example. Modify it as appropriate for a given product line, company, and circumstances. The format of objectives/strategies for the various marketing components is quite typical for a written plan, with rationale or justification included.

Target Market(s)

The first part of the action plan is the description of the target market. There will very likely be a primary target market as well as secondary targets developed from the market analysis in Chapter 5. The segments the product manager elects to target determine the marketing strategy as well as the product positioning and communication approaches. For example, Marvin Windows isolated different needs

Topic Outline	Description
Product Performance	Two to three paragraphs summarizing the product's performance relative to last year's plan, along with explanations of variances from the plan. Any research conducted on product performance or quality can be included in this section as well.
Background	Highlights from the background analysis, using bullet points as much as possible. It is useful to include the market analysis, competitive analysis, and/or performance history worksheets as attachments or exhibits.
Long-Term Objectives	A statement indicating the long-term direction for your product line and its long-term "fit" within the corporate strategic plan.
Problems/Opportunities	Problems that might make it difficult to achieve the objectives. List the steps to be taken to minimize the risk. Opportunities that will help in achieving the objectives.
Sales Forecasts/Goals	A statement of the product's forecasted sales for the next fiscal year. If there are several products or product lines to be examined separately, use a tabular format.
Marketing Objectives	Brief statements of objectives for the product or line for the next fiscal year. These can be stated in terms of revenue/profit, new-product trials, retention rates, etc.
Marketing Program	
1. Positioning statement	Use the positioning statement from Worksheet 7.1. Make sure that it lists the unique selling feature(s) of the product (i.e., how the product is to be perceived in the customer's mind relative to the competition). The positioning statement should be clear enough to be the "glue" for coordinating the subsequent marketing mix variables.
2. Target market(s)	Several paragraphs with a description of and rationale for the primary and secondary target markets.

Figure 7.2 Marketing Plan Outline

Topic Outline	Description
3. Product strategy	This section can contain several items, depending on the company and product requirements. There will be one or more objectives, each followed by a brief strategy statement. The format will usually be as follows: • Brief product description (such as one contained in a catalog) indicating the competitive differences, along with a table of the sizes and variety of products in the line. • Product objectives, including new uses, repositioning, line extensions/modifications, programs to improve quality, or new-product introductions. • Strategy • Rationale • Capacity utilization, including existing capacity along with manufacturing requirements of the marketing plan.
4. Pricing strategy	A general statement of the pricing strategy used for the product(s). Include any planned changes in price, discounts, warranties, and terms and conditions of sale, along with a table indicating the expected impact on selling and profit performance. The format will be as follows: • Brief description • Objective • Strategy • Rationale • Impact table
5. Advertising strategy a. National advertising	This section will have three components: 1. The competitive product differentiation to include in the advertising message. 2. The media plan along with a calendar of expected insertions. 3. Cost/spending information: • Brief description • Objective • Strategy

Figure 7.2 Marketing Plan Outline (continued)

Topic Outline	Description
	• Rationale • Implementation • Supporting tables
b. Cooperative advertising	A statement of the goals and general program description of cooperative advertising programs with channel members.
c. Trade advertising	If advertising to intermediaries who resell the product, the message and media plan should be summarized in this section.
6. Promotion strategy	There are several types of sales promotions, support materials, trade show plans, and other nonadvertising promotions that may be part of the marketing plan. These may be part of separate plans or strategy documents but should at least be summarized in this section. The format should be consistent with the others: • Objective • Strategy
7. Field sales plan	The field sales plan is almost always a separate planning document. Nevertheless, include any information that directly impacts the product or its marketing plan. For example, any training or incentive programs that are part of the budget or that are recommended in addition to the standard field sales plan should be included here.
8. Distribution strategy	Any recommendations regarding changes to the channel of distribution, including adding or deleting intermediaries, should be included. Also incorporate any programs necessary to motivate channel members or to collect information about the end-user from them. The format is as follows: • Objective • Strategy
9. Product support	Any recommendations regarding the warranty/guarantee for the product, customer service changes, or any other product support issues that affect the achievement of the product objectives. Maintain the format used earlier:

Figure 7.2 Marketing Plan Outline (continued)

Topic Outline	Description
	• Objective
	• Strategy
Training Requirements	Any training requirements (e.g., for customers) not included elsewhere in the marketing plan.
Marketing Research	Any planned research for the fiscal year, providing the proposal as an attachment.
Financial Summary	A pro forma profit and loss statement for the product(s). (See Figure 7.3.)
Schedules	An action schedule indicating who does what by when. Allow space for the appropriate individuals to sign and date their agreement to the stated tasks.

Figure 7.2 Marketing Plan Outline (continued)

among different segments of window buyers and advanced its position from eighth to third in the industry by stressing the most relevant benefits to each group. (See feature Segmentation at Marvin Windows.)

Part of the target market decision will also include the marshalling of resources to get the greatest impact for the marketing investment and to accomplish an objective such as being an industry leader. Industry leadership in the past meant being the biggest and having the most visible brands. Now, with markets fragmenting, leadership can be defined with a niche concept. By focusing a firm's resources on smaller segments, the firm becomes more visible and gains a perception of leadership in that segment.

> The most important insight . . . is the degree to which this whole concept validates the merits of a "niche" or "focus" strategy—seeking to become a large fish in a small pond. A brand of ice cream or beer carried in 500 retail outlets will benefit disproportionately . . . if all those outlets are in Iowa, not spread over the Midwest, and even more if they are in Des Moines. A business-to-business marketer can achieve the same level of visibility and "leadership position" by focus-

	Previous Year	Percent Sales	Current Year	Percent Sales	Next Year	Percent Sales
Product sales revenue	$		$		$	
Less price adjustments						
Cost of goods	— —		— —		— —	
Gross margin		%		%		%
Controllable marketing expenses						
Advertising						
Trade allowances						
Promotions						
Trade shows						
Sales support						
Training						
Total controllable marketing expenses	— —		— —		— —	
Product manager contribution margin		%		%		%
Other product expenses						
Sales force cost						
Distribution						
Administration						
Miscellaneous	— —		— —		— —	
Total other product expenses		%		%		%
Total expenses	— —		— —		— —	
Product contribution to overhead		%		%		%
Increase/decrease	%		%		%	

Figure 7.3 Profit and Loss Statement

ing on one industry. Becoming the leading supplier of inventory software for meatpackers may be not only a feasible objective, but also one that confers all the "snowball" benefits of brand leadership within that industry.[1]

Product Strategy

Several objectives in the product plan may be necessary to accomplish a stated sales forecast. For example, a product objective could be to attain sales of $X for each of three major products. The supporting

---

Segmentation at Marvin Windows

Marvin, a family-owned and controlled window manufacturer in War-road, Minnesota, discovered the value of market segmentation in reaching its customers more effectively. By studying buying processes, it identified builders, dealers, remodelers, and architects as influence groups and designed segment-specific advertising messages to reach them. For example, remodelers want windows that fit existing openings and don't require "customizing" the wall to fit a standard window. For this group, Marvin positioned itself as *the* made-to-order window manufacturer. In reaching building supply dealers, Marvin focused on a lowered need for inventory, thereby increasing dealer profitability. For builders and architects, Marvin emphasized its ability to meet both aesthetic and budgetary constraints.

Source: Adapted from Kate Bertrand, "Divide and Conquer," *Business Marketing* 74 (October 1989): 49–50.

---

strategy would explain what modifications this would require in terms of quality improvements, "bundling," or new uses. The rationale would explain why this is possible given the background analysis.

Branding and packaging might or might not be a crucial part of the plan, but they should at least be considered. Be sure that the customer need is addressed and explain why a specific product satisfies this need better than the competition does. Also, mention the effect of other products on the product line and/or the effect of the line on the company product mix.

New-product plans might be separate because they usually cover a different time period from the annual plan. However, because they impact a product manager's bottom line, they should probably be summarized here. New-product specifications, positioning, budget, and event schedules can be included. (See Part III for more information on product strategies and tactics.)

Pricing Strategy

The pricing section should start with a statement of general company policies and how specific product pricing fits within those policies. Any changes in discounts, price packages, warranties, terms and conditions of sale, or any other variables should be listed, along with an explanation of the impact on the profitability of the line and of the "fit" in the overall positioning and product strategy. (See Chapters 11 and 12 for more information on pricing.)

Advertising Strategy

The advertising section could be quite long if several types of advertising are used. The national (or regional) advertising directed at the end-customer would require a different message and media than does advertising directed at the trade. Therefore, separate campaigns will need to be developed. In any case, the product manager must make sure the media and messages are coordinated to match the positioning statement and overall marketing objectives stated in the annual plan.

The media planning part of the strategy should list, in calendar format, the media vehicles used to convey the message. (See Figure 7.4.) The rationale should explain why this mix of media and insertions would accomplish the reach/frequency/cost goals of the campaign. (See Chapter 13 for more information on advertising.)

Promotion Strategy

Sales promotion refers to tools, other than advertising, used to stimulate short-term demand. This includes coupons, free samples, contests, premiums, point-of-purchase material, and so on. Customer, trade, and sales force promotions can be included in this section, along with budgets and calendars (similar to the examples mentioned previously).

Sales support materials can be covered in this section or in the field sales section. Also, any trade show strategies, merchandising, or publicity that the company is involved in should be addressed.

Field Sales Plan

The field sales plan is usually beyond a product manager's control, but there might be activities for which product managers are responsible or

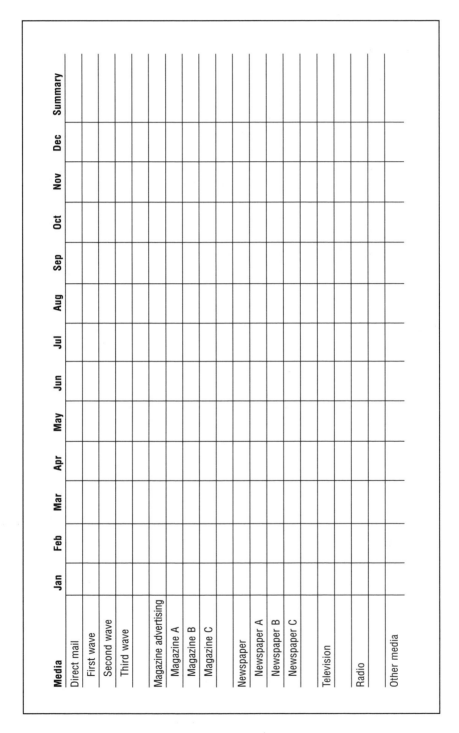

Media	Jan	Feb	Mar	Apr	May	Jun	Jul	Aug	Sep	Oct	Nov	Dec	Summary
Direct mail													
First wave													
Second wave													
Third wave													
Magazine advertising													
Magazine A													
Magazine B													
Magazine C													
Newspaper													
Newspaper A													
Newspaper B													
Newspaper C													
Television													
Radio													
Other media													

Figure 7.4 Media Calendar

activities that must be performed to attain product goals. In those cases, they should be included in this portion of the annual marketing plan.

Distribution Strategy

The distribution strategy section should contain a statement on general policies and the desired penetration or coverage. If there are any planned changes, such as adding/deleting intermediaries or creating programs to improve relationships, they should be mentioned here along with the "fit" into the positioning and overall marketing objectives.

Product Support

The product support section should provide a general statement on the policies for warranty/guarantee and repair service as well as any anticipated changes. As always, this should be coordinated with the rest of the marketing program so that the positioning and marketing objectives are achieved.

Checklist: Hints on Writing the
Annual Product Marketing Plan

✓ Word your annual product marketing objectives so that they indicate what you want to accomplish during the next fiscal year to take advantage of identified opportunities and to overcome potential problems.

✓ Be sure the objectives are consistent with the long-term vision of the product line and company.

✓ Identify the group(s) of customers you are going to focus your energies and resources on during the next fiscal year. This becomes your target market(s).

✓ Since many competitors could be going after this same group of customers, use your positioning statement to explain how you want customers to view you as better than the competition and how you can provide evidence of this difference.

✓ Consider the impact that pricing, advertising, field selling, distribution strategy, and product support have on one another as well as on the success of your product. Write the marketing plan with these impacts in mind.

Case Two[1]

The Importance of Data

MARKETING PLANS CAN be effective only if based on a realistic analysis of data. If they are not, they are simply budgets with opinions. Product managers collect and maintain data for the marketing plan in a product fact book, a compendium providing the nuts and bolts of the planning process. (See Chapter 8.) This case describes the product fact book Colgate-Palmolive uses in its product rollouts, and then summarizes the key points in the marketing planning process for Chrysler's Neon.

Colgate-Palmolive's Bundle Book

Colgate-Palmolive has adapted the idea of a product fact book into what it calls a bundle book—a three-ring binder containing everything the company knows about a product or category—and uses it to create global brands. The bundle book is distributed to Colgate subsidiaries to provide consistency and uniformity in rolling out brands to different regions.

According to Sharen Kindel in "Selling by the Book" (*Sales & Marketing Management*), Colgate's bundle books provide descriptive plans for a product roll-out:

> Bundle books contain such information as: a product overview, a definition of the marketing opportunity, the product's uniqueness, a vision statement, the product family, a digest of consumer research, packaging, graphics, and pricing strategy. Also included are the advertising plan, support materials, a professional relations program, information pertaining to advertising claim substantiation, and even specific advertising executions. The book will answer questions regarding such technical issues as the formula, additives, fragrance, color and stability and provide a list of key contacts to check information or answer questions. Says John Steele [head of global business development], "We send the subsidiaries the kind of advertising we want. They're tested ads that are already working in some markets." Detailed country profiles provide specifics on the rollout plan and how the brand has performed to date. Information on competitive brands and their advertising support is also included.

The bundle books can be 150 to 200 pages in length and in some situations can exceed one volume. When Colgate launched its Colgate

Total toothpaste in 1993, the launch was preceded by eighteen months of research, resulting in a two-volume book. One volume contained the results of test marketing in six countries, carefully selected to provide a representative range of countries facing different marketing opportunities and constraints. The second volume covered public relations and advertising claim substantiation. Advertising, packaging, pricing, and positioning were consistent among all subsidiaries. Using the bundle book, Colgate's subsidiaries were able to launch Total in sixty-six countries within two years, the fastest global launch in Colgate's history.

The material in Colgate's bundle book provides the essence of the background analysis for product marketing planning as well as details about the action program. Although Colgate emphasizes its use for global new-product rollouts, the basic concepts are appropriate for annual planning and domestic strategies as well.

The *business assessment* coincides with the general culture of the company and its impact on the plan. In Colgate's case, the books were in line with the centralized marketing philosophy of the company. Colgate prefers to give direction to its subsidiaries, whereas one of its major competitors, Unilever, allows its subsidiaries more freedom in the use of specific marketing tactics.

The *market analysis* focuses on selecting the appropriate customers for allocation of resources. For Colgate, the bundle books provide a consistent way of looking at the market—even small, fragmented markets. They provide input on the demographic and psychographic profiles of consumers most likely to use the products. This helps subsidiaries uncover new segments that are highly profitable or are underserved by the competition.

The *competitive strategy* depends on Colgate's relative position within a category. Since toothpaste is a core product for Colgate, the launch of Total required global speed to preempt competitors from bringing out a competing product and limiting its effectiveness. In the bleach category, a different approach was necessary. Colgate had just recently entered this business through acquisitions. Therefore, the competitive portion of the bundle book contained new information to educate employees. The competitive portion should identify the competitors' general strategies, product differentiation, future moves, and consumer perceptions.

The *performance history*, since Colgate's bundle books focus on new products, contains test market results. Colgate tested Total in Australia, Columbia, Greece, the Philippines, Portugal, and the United Kingdom. The information gathered on sampling, the use of television, and other variables were incorporated into the bundle book. For these books to be used for annual marketing planning, it would be necessary to compare planned versus actual sales figures, along with the related analysis of why they occurred.

Trends also played a role in Colgate's strategy. In the past, when there were few global brands and limited international technology, there was little need for a standardized approach to megabrands. Now, with the trend toward instantaneous communication (fax, electronic mail, or overnight courier can transmit information virtually anywhere in the world), providing a common brand strategy using a bundle book becomes valuable.

Key Points in Marketing Planning for the Chrysler Neon

Chrysler also went through significant analysis prior to developing the marketing plan for the Neon, its subcompact car. A brief summary of the key points is presented here, using the format from the chapters in Part II.

Background Analysis

The business assessment—the evaluation of Chrysler as a company—is the first part of the background analysis. Chrysler had both positive and negative points relative to marketing a subcompact car. First, it demonstrated stronger progress in improving its product development process than was true for the other American companies. This increased the likelihood of controlling development costs, thereby producing an affordable car. Second, it was committed to bringing out a successful small car and had, in fact, considered a joint deal with Fiat.

On the negative side, Chrysler had the worst quality record of the Big Three. Its prior attempts to enter the small-car market were dismal. In 1992 the Dodge Shadow and Plymouth Sundance had 162 problems and 137 problems, respectively, per 100 cars, according to J. D. Power. The only car with a worse record was the Hyundai Excel.

The *market analysis* was favorable. Both the domestic and foreign markets represented growing potential for subcompacts. Marketing research among current subcompact owners showed they wanted a small car that felt like a big one yet was fun to drive, safe, and reliable. Young families viewed this type of car as a utility vehicle. In terms of features, customers indicated a willingness to forego power windows and a four-speed automatic transmission in exchange for a reasonable price (base price approximately $9,000). Nevertheless, safety was paramount.

There were several *competitors* on the market, but they were generally higher-cost producers. Ford's new Escort, developed with Mazda, took five years to develop at a cost of $2 billion. When it was introduced, it turned out to be a rough-riding car, causing Ford to start selling it at $9,995 (a $500 loss per car according to analysts). Saturn was a formidable competitor, but with seven years of development the cost was estimated at $5 billion. Japanese subcompacts still had a high-quality image, but the average costs in 1993 were 13 percent more than in 1991, with a related market share drop from 52 percent to 49 percent. The competitive comparison as presented in *Business Week* in early 1993 is shown in Figure 7.5.

Since the Neon had not yet been introduced, there were no sales, quality, or other *performance measures* to track. However, prelaunch checks were extensive. Test drivers logged unprecedented hours, with several early prototypes achieving 250,000 miles.

Trends were also favorable for the Neon. Federal mileage standards were expected to rise, forcing the automotive companies to increase their development of cars with good gas mileage. Also, the recession spurred more interest in smaller, affordable cars.

Synthesis

An examination of the background analysis yielded several problems and opportunities. A primary challenge to overcome was the American market's perception that Chrysler products had low quality. This would need to be attacked by incorporating extra quality features into the car and using marketing communications effectively to combat the image. Chrysler also realized that they could attain their target price

	Price	Base engine/ horsepower	Weight in pounds	Fuel mpg	Driver air bags	Passenger air bags
Neon	$8,600–$12,500	2 liter/130	2,300	30+ (est)	standard	standard
Honda Civic	$8,950–$16,080	1.5 liter/102	2,300	38	standard	optional
Ford Escort	$8,335–$11,923	1.9 liter/88	2,300	33	N/A	N/A
GM Saturn	$9,395–$13,570	1.9 liter/85	2,300	36	standard	N/A
Nissan Sentra	$8,995–$15,020	1.6 liter/110	2,400	35	optional	N/A
Toyota Tercel	$7,998–$12,038	1.5 liter/82	2,000	29	standard	N/A

Figure 7.5 Neon's Competitive Features

and still be profitable only if sales approached their capacity of 300,000 cars per year. This figure was well above any competing subcompact sales figures, but the company had to shoot for this goal to make the project successful at the target price.

Based on that information, the Neon marketing objective was to sell 300,000 cars, of which 10 percent would be at base price. The domestic models would be available January 1994, with European models rolling out four months later in April. The positioning approach would be reminiscent of the Volkswagen Beetle positioning in the early 1960s. The Neon would be positioned as "youthful, lively, and a little bit huggable," a functional car at a good price.

Action Program

The primary target market was "Generation X," individuals in the eighteen-to-thirty-two-year-old range, earning in the mid-$20,000s; college students were part of this segment. Boomers over thirty with income in the low $40,000s formed a secondary market. These groups were somewhat cynical and hard to sell to, but were consistent with the positioning of functional value.

The product, the Neon itself, was designed to appeal to the described target market, to attack the quality perception, and to achieve the target price. The Neon has a long wheelbase (seven inches longer than the Toyota Corolla) to allow more room in the rear seat. The cab-forward look allowed a high roof to be carried over the passenger compartment to provide more front and back headroom. These features provided the big-car "feel" the marketing research indicated was important to future customers. To attack the issue of safety, Neon became the first subcompact with standard dual air bags. It also incorporated reinforced doors to meet the 1997 federal side-impact standard, anti-lock brakes on all models, and height-adjustable front belts. In terms of achieving the target price, the base Neon was designed with crank windows and similar spartan features, consistent with input from consumers.

The base price was approximately $9,457, ringing in at $850 less than the cheapest four-door Saturn. However, several option packages allowed a "nicely loaded" Neon to be available for $11,000 to $13,000. A popularly equipped version would cost about $12,000, with a Sport model carrying a $13,000 price tag.

Early promotional strategies relied heavily on advance publicity. News articles in business and consumer publications, test-drive reports from automotive journalists and industry analysts, and various feature stories provided credible support for Chrysler's product development process and renewed control over quality. An estimated $80 million was budgeted for the marketing campaign. BBDO, the advertising agency for the product, broke the debut campaign on the Super Bowl. A blizzard of billboard ads near dealers pictured the front of the car with the simple headline, "Hi," to bring to life the desired positioning of "youthful, lively, and a little bit huggable." Television, radio, and print advertising were consistent with and reinforced the message on the billboards. Care was taken to avoid pigeonholing the younger generation. Instead of using MTV-style advertising or stereotyping Generation X, the campaign focused on communicating product benefits while developing a huggable personality for the car.

The distribution strategy was to sell the Neon under the same brand name to both Dodge and Plymouth dealers. This tactic was intended to reinforce to the cynical target market that Chrysler wasn't using superficial differentiation to sell the car through the two separate dealer networks. By creating a single model name, Neon, in effect, became the brand. This approach enabled the company to get more benefit from its advertising investment.

Part III

PRODUCT SKILLS

M ost product managers have responsibility for both existing and new products. For existing products, the product manager is expected to (1) maintain a database or fact book, (2) evaluate product performance, (3) add value, (4) increase market penetration, and (5) evaluate the product line.

The ongoing product analysis, along with external input on the customers and competition, will trigger ideas for line extensions and totally new concepts. The process of turning these ideas into commercially viable products is often a company endeavor that is coordinated by the product manager. He or she can play a vital role in idea generation, screening, concept development and testing, prototype testing, prelaunch, launch, and project evaluation.

Part III addresses the analytical skills a product manager needs to evaluate an existing product line, as well as to determine and implement new-product strategies.

8

Evaluating the Product Portfolio

MUCH OF A product manager's time is spent evaluating and improving on existing products and on modifications of the product line. Even if the product is the same for a while, the marketing strategy might need to change. A routine examination of the product line should uncover the types of changes necessary for optimizing the company's product position. If a product manager is responsible for a limited number of products, it might be possible to conduct thorough analyses of each. However, the reality for most companies is that the Pareto rule applies: 80 percent of the sales and/or profits come from 20 percent of the products. These most important products should have constant attention, with the rest receiving periodic attention.

There are five activities the product manager should perform relative to evaluating the product portfolio (See Figure 8.1). First, the product manager must maintain (or establish) a database of relevant information on the product. Second, the products must be evaluated in terms of customer satisfaction, competition, and company expectations. Third, the product manager must add value to existing products by improving features, adding an element of competitive superiority, and/or reducing costs. Fourth, the product manager should attempt to increase market penetration by appealing to more users or increasing the usage rate of existing customers. And, finally, the product manager must evaluate the product line to look for gaps where new products need to be developed and/or to determine when to delete products.

1. Establish and maintain a database of relevant information on the product, the market, and the competition.
2. Evaluate key products in terms of customer satisfaction, competitive advantages, and company expectations.
3. Add value by improving features and/or reducing costs.
4. Increase market penetration by identifying new uses and new users.
5. Look for gaps in the product line.

Figure 8.1 Activities of Managing Existing Products

Maintain a Database on Existing Products (the "Product Fact Book")

The product manager's first job related to evaluating the product portfolio is to ensure that product-related information is in a form conducive to analysis and decision making. This is the *product fact book*, where all relevant information is in a central location. The information in the fact book can be held in a three-ring binder, a manual filing system, or an electronic database.

There is no one right way to set up a database; it depends on the needs of the product manager. Typically, there will be files on customer profiles and changes, the perceived importance of various product features, the major competitors and their strengths and weaknesses, the sales/profit/contribution history of the product or product line, and technological or macroeconomic trends that could impact product sales in the future.

The information in the database must be updated periodically through marketing research, input from the customer service department, input from the sales force, on-line database searching, and/or published information from trade publications. As noted in Case Two, following Chapter 7, the product fact book provides the data necessary for ongoing decisions as well as for much of the background analysis for annual marketing plans and product launches.

Evaluate Product Performance

The beginning point for a product performance evaluation is the audit conducted as part of the performance history portion of the background analysis (see Chapter 5). This should have triggered problems and opportunities related to features, potential new-product entries, and/or quality issues that should be addressed in the product plan for the upcoming fiscal year. Aspects to evaluate about product performance include sales/profits by customer segment, channel of distribution, or geographic region; the complementary value of the product to others in the line; seasonal fluctuations in demand; the awareness and preference level for the product; rate of repeat purchases (retention); and the planned-to-actual performance.

Product managers should avoid thinking about existing products as mature, but should rather treat them as "core brands." Think about the brands as if they were being acquired from another company; envision the possibilities. Study customers to find out not only their buyer behavior, but also what causes that behavior.[1]

Product managers frequently use competitive matrices to study their products. A competitive matrix is a visual display of one product versus the competition along two axes. Each axis is a continuum of an attribute such as ease of use, comfort, or price. The selection of attributes should be based on what is important to customers.

A competitive matrix (sometimes called a perceptual map) focuses attention on the relative competitive positioning a product has along significant factors. (See Figure 8.2.) Start by determining what is most important to a customer in making a buying decision. Ask customers to list and rank attributes in terms of priority and to assess how significant those attributes truly are in terms of affecting their purchase decisions.

Then select the top two or four attributes to utilize for the relative positioning of significant competitors along each attribute. For example, assume that Product A is compared with competing products X, Y, and Z along two important purchase criteria: leadership in the market and ease of use. Note that A is perceived as a leader to a greater degree than the competition; this could be used as part of its positioning strategy. However, it is also perceived as more difficult to use

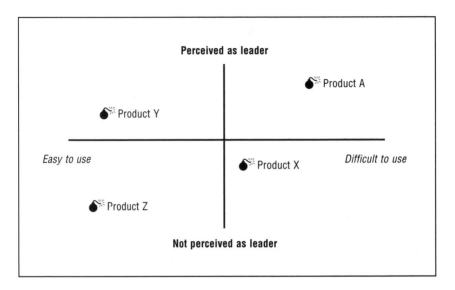

Figure 8.2 Competitive Matrix (Perceptual Map)

than any of the competitors. This could suggest a strategy of providing clearer instructions and/or redesigning the product to make it easier to use.

Another approach to this, when several factors are deemed equally important, is to list all factors as continua (as bipolar adjectives along a scale, like *light* to *heavy*) and ask customers to rate each product along each factor. The average or mean responses for each competitive product can be joined by a line to indicate a "profile" of each. In Figure 8.3, three products are being evaluated against one another. Product A is perceived as slightly superior in terms of product consistency, Product B is easiest to use, and Product C has better delivery.

Add Value to Existing Products

Both the competitive matrix and profile approaches just described compare a product against its competitors along established factors. The typical objective is to improve attributes that are competitively weak. What is generally missing is the internal cost of the specific factors. Sometimes a product can be made more profitable by reducing the cost

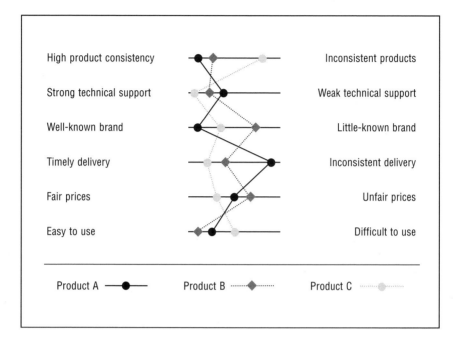

High product consistency — Inconsistent products

Strong technical support — Weak technical support

Well-known brand — Little-known brand

Timely delivery — Inconsistent delivery

Fair prices — Unfair prices

Easy to use — Difficult to use

Product A ——●——   Product B ·····◆·····   Product C ·····◉·····

Figure 8.3 Comparative Product Scaling

of unimportant attributes. If this also results in a price reduction, the result can be more value to the customer. Therefore, it is useful to add cost information to the perceived importance and competitive performance of each attribute, as shown in Figure 8.4.

Note that the first column of Figure 8.4 shows features and attributes of the product. These have to be converted to benefits in the second column. The average importance of each benefit to the market must be determined (through marketing research) or estimated (from informal customer input) and listed in the third column. The next column indicates how well the product supplies the benefit relative to the competition. The final column indicates whether the cost of the related features is a significant proportion of the overall cost of the product.

Look for red flags in the table. The provision of benefits that are highly important to the market should be from features that are at least equal to or better than the competition in terms of performance. If that is not the case, the product manager should improve on those fea-

Features/ Attributes	Benefits	Importance to Market	Competitive Performance	Relative Cost

Figure 8.4 Costs and Benefits of Features
Relative to the Market Importance

tures. If features provide benefits that are not important to the customer, the relative cost should be low. Otherwise, the feature should be eliminated or provided at as low a cost as possible.

This type of analysis should precede quality improvement and cost reduction programs. By working with teams from other parts of the company, the product manager can use value analysis, quality function deployment, or other techniques to increase customer satisfaction without a commensurate increase in costs or maintain customer satisfaction while lowering costs.

It is important to continually rethink and redefine the product creatively to look for opportunities hidden behind the day-to-day grind. (See Figure 8.5.)What would happen if some features were magnified? For example, magnifying the screen on a television created a new market for home theater. Similarly, *reducing* the screen created sports TVs.

What if a new feature replaced an old one? For example, Sony created the Walkman by replacing speakers with a headset. Can two existing products be combined to provide one with more value to the customer? The minivan combined the advantages of a station wagon with those of a van. Sometimes two product managers can bundle their products together to create more value than selling either one separately to the customer.

Can certain elements be modified? This could include both product features and ancillary services. Sometimes industries become so embroiled in "that's the way we've always done it" that modifications to sales approaches, contract terms, or other things are overlooked.

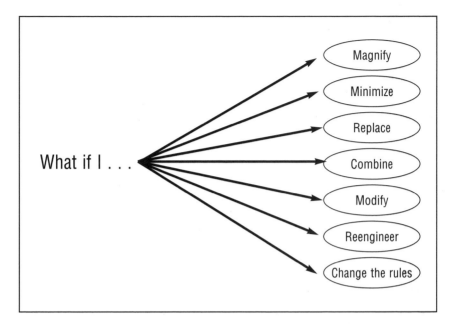

Figure 8.5 Rethinking Your Product

Can the development process be reengineered to reduce the overall cost of producing the product or service? Can the traditional approach be changed: for example, can direct mail or the Internet be used as an alternative to the traditional method of distributing the product?

After identifying features that deserve detailed examination, the next job of the product manager is to benchmark these features against the "best-in-class." Start by finding out from salespeople, customers, and industry writings what company or product is recognized as best for the aspect under study. Then strive to uncover why it is perceived as best. For example, when Ford redesigned the 1992 Taurus, it benchmarked more than two hundred features against seven competitors. Door handles were benchmarked against the Chevy Lumina, headlamps against the Accord, and remote radio controls against the Pontiac Grand Prix.[2]

However, benchmarking should not be limited to the competition, and it does not have to be limited to product features. By improving processes used to deliver a product or service, it is possible to provide more value for the customer. Mellon Bank in Pittsburgh, for example, undertook a benchmarking project to improve its credit card billing practices. By benchmarking seven other companies, including an airline, they learned about techniques and software technologies to improve the process. After adopting several improvements, they cut outstanding complaints by half and were able to resolve problems in an average of twenty-five days instead of the forty-five days it took previously.[3]

Increase Market Penetration

Another tactic the product manager could use is to boost sales volume by increasing the number of users and/or the usage rate per user. The number of users can be increased by winning competitors' customers, entering new market segments, and/or converting nonusers into users. Volume can also be increased by finding new applications for the product or by encouraging more frequent usage.

To increase the number of users, a product manager must collect three types of information: (1) why competitors' customers buy from the competition; (2) what, if anything, could convince nonusers to become users of the product; and (3) what market segments are attractive and accessible. Information for the first two items on the list can be obtained partly through sales input in the way of lost order reports. However, this is at best an incomplete picture, because not all customers are contacted by the sales force. Therefore, if this is critical data, some additional research is necessary. Focus groups and one-on-one interviews can uncover new insights into why customers choose alternative products or choose none at all.

To identify what segments are attractive and accessible requires a combination of information and intuition. Start by profiling existing customer segments that have shown higher than average increases in sales. Determine whether these increases are unique to the product's customers or whether noncustomers with similar profiles have also exhibited a need for the product. Then assess whether the total segment (customers and noncustomers) is growing or declining in sheer size. Also look for segments that have suddenly appeared and have specific needs not being addressed by the competition.

Evaluate the Product Line

In evaluating a product line, the product manager can use the same steps discussed in this chapter previously, particularly when the line is

	Competitor A's product line	Competitor B's product line	Your product line
Fail-safe resistors	x		x
Nonpolarized chip		x	
Voltage regulator	x	x	x
Flat chip resistor	x	x	x
Brackets	x	x	
27-inch yoke	x		x

Figure 8.6 Product-Line Comparison

comprised of fast-moving consumer goods (FMCG). First, data need to be maintained on each item in the line. Second, relative product performance needs to be evaluated. This includes an examination of customer behavior for the entire line. Try to determine whether customers can substitute a filler product if the core product is out of stock or whether they are apt to buy a competing product. Third, increase value to the product line by (a) adding products that enhance the competitive positioning and increase brand equity or (b) deleting products that are not important to the target market and simply increase costs. Finally, increase market penetration by generating more usage through a carefully planned marketing communications strategy.

Regularly evaluate the product line to look for gaps to be filled or products to be eliminated. A starting point may be to compare your product line to competing product lines to highlight potential gaps or to uncover potentially unnecessary products. (See Figure 8.6.) Note that in the example shown in Figure 8.6, yours is the only product line in the competitive set not carrying brackets. This could make installation more difficult, causing a potential competitive disadvantage.

Product managers frequently use portfolio matrices as visual tools to compare products within a line. A common matrix is the product-market attractiveness model developed by General Electric working with McKinsey & Co. (See Figure 8.7.) This matrix groups products into nine categories, along some combination of business strength and

Figure 8.7 Product-Market Attractiveness

market attractiveness. Products are evaluated as low, medium, or high in terms of business strength and market attractiveness. Business strength includes items such as whether the particular product is a core product of the company based on its competencies, the market share of the particular product, and the profitability of the product. Market attractiveness includes such factors as market growth rate, competitiveness within the product category, and strategic importance of the market to the company.

In Figure 8.7, products in the "1" cells have a strong position and should be enhanced through additional investment. Products in the "3" cells are weak and should be evaluated carefully to determine whether there is significant complementary value to retain them or whether they should be dropped. If a product elimination is being considered, there must be a careful examination of overhead cost absorption. Sometimes a weak product is at least covering all direct costs and contributing to overhead. If it is dropped, it is possible that the overhead would be allocated to other products, possibly making them marginal as well. Products in the "2" cells are questionable, and money should be invested selectively in them.

The matrix in Figure 8.7 is simply an example of one that any company could develop. Choose the variables of most importance in evaluating the line and determine the best way to categorize the existing products. If your company does not have a product-review committee, recommend that one be established. The committee should be comprised of representatives from marketing, manufacturing, and finance. The committee should develop a company-appropriate system for identifying weak products. The system would specify how frequently to meet (e.g., quarterly, annually), what criteria to examine (number of quarters of sales decline, market changes, gross margin, etc.), and procedures for product elimination. Whatever recommendations are made should be included in the annual plan with rationale and a statement of the impact on the overall marketing program.

Checklist: Tips on Evaluating the Product Portfolio

✓ Before evaluating your products in depth, prioritize them in terms of their profitability and strategic potential. Practice the 80/20 rule.

✓ Collect and maintain information on your products, your customers, and your competition on an ongoing basis.

✓ Determine the features or attributes of your product (including supporting services) of highest importance to your customers; then regularly compare these against the best-in-class products and companies.

✓ Don't limit your analysis to what customers say is important now; challenge yourself to rethink and redefine the product to uncover hidden opportunities for the future.

✓ Remember that the markets for your products aren't static; look for new ways to increase users and usage.

✓ In addition to examining individual products, study the total product line or mix you offer your customers. Weed out weak products and add new products to fill in the gaps as appropriate.

9

Strategic Product Planning

STRATEGIC PRODUCT PLANNING requires an understanding of corporate and divisional strategic goals. Most long-term visions have some implicit (or explicit) statement of the future "picture" of the company and its product offerings. The product manager has to understand the role his or her product(s) play in this vision. It is not enough to know the percentage of profits expected from a new-product line, although that is important information. The product manager must also know what new markets, new technologies, and new directions should be incorporated into the long-term product plan.

Strategic product thinking is different from new-product development (discussed in Chapter 10), because it forces product managers to envision a future that does not yet exist to lead the market and create products before customers ask for them. This requires a certain level of risk and creativity. Product managers must ask themselves: How will the customers of tomorrow be different from the customers of today? What products/services will these customers expect? What existing capabilities can we expect to use in the future and what new abilities will we need to develop? The emphasis is not on projecting the present into the future. Rather, the emphasis is on trying to understand how the future will be different from the present and the impact that will have on present planning.

Fostering a Customer Mind-Set

Fostering a customer mind-set requires the product manager to step back and redefine the business in terms of customer functions. It may also require redefining what it means to satisfy the customer. When David Whitwam became CEO of Whirlpool, his vision was to transform the company into a customer-focused organization and to shift thinking from product to customer, as indicated in the following excerpt from an interview in *Harvard Business Review*:

> The starting point isn't the existing product; it's the function consumers buy products to accomplish. When you return to first principles, the design issues dramatically change. The microwave couldn't have been invented by someone who assumed he or she was in the business of designing a range. Such a design breakthrough required seeing that the opportunity is "easier, quicker food preparation," not "a better range."
>
> Take the "fabric-care business," which we used to call the "washing-machine business." We're now studying consumer behavior from the time people take off their dirty clothes at night until they've been cleaned and ironed and hung in the closet. What are we looking for? The worst part of the process is not the washing and drying. The hard part is when you take your clothes out of the dryer and you have to do something with them—iron, fold, hang them up. Whoever comes up with a product to make this part of the process easier, simpler, or quicker is going to create an incredible market.[1]

Before continuing this section on strategic product planning, complete the quiz "Assessing Your Company's Strategic IQ," shown in Figure 9.1.

Understanding Past Successes and Failures

Another step in strategic evaluation is to calculate your company's "hit rate" in new products and determine the reasons for it. Compare successful product launches with unsuccessful ones. What were the common elements of successful development efforts that were different from unsuccessful development efforts? Was there a difference in R & D investment and shared communication? The number of ideas generated? The sequence of steps in the development process? The understanding of the market? The application of core competencies? All of

Read each of the following questions; evaluate your firm on a 1–5 scale (for questions 1–10) or a 1–10 scale (for questions 11–15), with 1 = Poor and the top value (5 or 10) = Excellent.

_____1. The company has a directional vision or "picture" of what it will look like in the future.

_____2. The strategic vision is stated concisely to avoid overloading the organization with competing (and possibly conflicting) initiatives.

_____3. Strategic thinking (broad-based, unrestricted) coexists with strategic planning (narrower and more detailed in focus).

_____4. The company emphasizes leveraging its resources to move toward an ambitious vision rather than restricting its vision to fit *current* resources.

_____5. In making outsourcing, divestiture, and product elimination decisions, the impact of the decision on distinctive competencies is considered.

_____6. In making acquisition decisions, the impact on core capabilities is considered.

_____7. There is a competitive focus throughout the organization and a widespread use of competitive intelligence.

_____8. The company uses competitive *innovation* at least as frequently as (if not more frequently than) competitive *imitation.*

_____9. Key members in all departments throughout the company are aware of market trends that could impact the strategy.

_____10. The strategic plan plays an integral role in the development of annual marketing plans.

Note: The next five questions are worth 10 points each.

_____11. The company has studied its historical track record to truly understand the abilities and processes that drive its competitive edge.

_____12. The company strives for a portfolio of competitive advantages rather than simply a portfolio of products.

_____13. Annual plans do not simply project the past and present into the future, but rather describe what must be done (perhaps differently) next year to move closer to the strategic vision.

_____14. The company strives to transform its key processes into strategic capabilities that consistently provide *superior value to the customer.*

_____15. New products developed indicate that the company knows what customers want before customers know it themselves.

_____ **Total** (100 points)

Figure 9.1 Assessing Your Company's Strategic IQ

these can be significant factors and must be part of the strategic thinking process.

Research & development and manufacturing personnel are important contributors to successful strategic product planning. Product managers should determine with manufacturing how wide a product line can be without putting a strain on efficiency. This includes understanding how future products can be developed from a common platform. Prevent product proliferation by deciding which products can be dropped when new ones are introduced. If products are not to be dropped, the product manager must lobby for increased R & D and/or operations support to attain the strategic product goals.

Developing Product Ideas

The number of ideas generated can affect successful product commercialization by increasing the likelihood of uncovering the best product concepts. Although many argue that there is no shortage of ideas per se, it can also be argued that many good ideas never surface because the available ideas are "good enough." Product managers are frequently under pressure to generate new products quickly. Because they also juggle existing products at the same time, they do not allow themselves the luxury of thoroughly examining all alternatives. They resort to line extensions or "me-too" products because thinking is muddied by the present. That is why strategic gestation of ideas can be a useful prelude to product development.

There are several sources of strategic product ideas. An important source is customers and potential customers. Unfortunately, too many companies don't use a disciplined approach to obtain futuristic ideas. For business-to-business products, a useful research approach is a systematic customer visit program. A customer visit program is a structured approach to data collection through which specific customers are targeted for their expected contributions to an issue being studied, company personnel are recruited to participate in the program due to their importance to the decision being made, and written objectives are established for the data collection. Customers who are future-thinkers, who are industry leaders, or who have unique applications for the product are asked to participate in the program. A small group of people from R & D, operations, and marketing are briefed on the goal of the project, and arrangements are made to call on the selected customers. The resulting insights from the customer visit program are then synthesized into potential long-term product ideas. Trade shows are another vehicle for reaching customers. Conducting a focus group at a trade show can be a lower-cost alternative for obtaining new product ideas.

Brainstorming sessions focused on a particular goal can also be a valuable tool for product development. During the session, participants are encouraged to think in terms of metaphors and analogies. The application of analogies was used successfully when Canon was attempting to develop a disposable drum for its minicopiers.

> Canon designers knew that for the first personal copier to be successful, it had to be reliable. To ensure reliability, they proposed to make the product's photosensitive copier drum—which is the source of 90 percent of all maintenance problems—disposable. To be disposable, however, the drum would have to be easy and cheap to make. How to manufacture a throwaway drum?
>
> The breakthrough came one day when task-force leader Hiroshi Tanaka ordered out for some beer. As the team discussed design problems over their drinks, Tanaka held one of the beer cans and wondered aloud, "How much does it cost to manufacture this can?" The question led the team to speculate whether the same process for making an aluminum beer can could be applied to the manufacture of an aluminum copier drum. By exploring how the drum actually is and is not like a beer can, the minicopier development team was able to come up with the process technology that could manufacture an aluminum drum at the appropriate low cost.[2]

Product managers must also be aware of the company's core competencies and be willing to work with other functional areas and other product managers to leverage these skills into future products and markets. (See feature Strategic Leveraging at 3M and Hewlett-Packard.) Rubbermaid, for example, encourages its employees to focus on the abilities of other parts of the company and use them if possible in their areas:

> Rubbermaid teaches its people to let ideas flow out of its so-called core competencies, the things it does best. Bud Hellman, who used to run a Rubbermaid subsidiary, was touring one of the company's picnic-cooler plants in the late Eighties when he suddenly realized he could use its plastic blow-molding techniques to make a durable, light-

weight, and inexpensive line of office furniture. The result was the WorkManager System, which the company says accounts for 60 percent of its furniture division sales. Says Charles Hassel, a member of the product development team: "If top management hadn't encouraged us to look at processes and technologies elsewhere in the company, none of this would have ever happened."[3]

Targeting Current, Tangential, and New Markets

Products can have varying levels of risk, and it is usually wise to have a portfolio of new products to balance the risk/return equation. New products with the lowest risk are line extensions—slight modifications (New and improved! versions) of an existing product. Larger or smaller package sizes, stronger or weaker flavors, and lighter or heavier components are all examples of line extensions. Most of these modifications are intended to increase usage among or provide more options for current customers. Sometimes the same (or a slightly different) product can be repositioned to attain usage among tangential markets. The classic example of this is baking soda, which was repositioned for numerous applications beyond baking. Bayer pain reliever extended to five models to increase usage among tangential markets such as people with arthritis or heart-attack victims. Finally, taking the existing product to a new market can be potentially profitable, but it must be marketed correctly. For example, the Bendix Brake Division of Allied Signal wanted to increase its brake sales in the do-it-yourself (DIY) market. It discovered that its packaging didn't connote high quality, so it redesigned its packaging to incorporate a strong color blue as part of the repositioning strategy. In one year its sales moved from less than 1 percent market share to more than 20 percent.

Products that are more than line extensions are also new and can be marketed to the same customer segments, tangential segments, or totally new markets. Of these three alternatives, the least risky is reaching the existing customer base through franchise extensions. A franchise extension (also referred to as a brand extension) refers to taking what the product (or brand) connotes and applying it in a different product category. For example, Arm & Hammer baking soda extended its brand franchise to detergent, toothpaste, and similar products for which the concept of "clean and fresh" was appropriate. Castle &

Strategic Leveraging at 3M and Hewlett-Packard

Both 3M and Hewlett-Packard are recognized leaders in innovation and strategic product planning. Their success is due to several factors. An important one is the ability to leverage skills across divisions and into new market applications. Another is cannibalizing products before someone else does.

Going beyond cross-functional to cross-divisional thinking, 3M's CEO, L. D. DeSimone, is urging his R & D teams to apply proprietary technology wherever it can work. For example, focus group input suggested that consumers did not like the fact that steel wool soap pads rusted and frayed. Staff from both the tape and abrasives divisions worked together to create the Never Rust Wool Soap Pad, using fibers from recycled plastic bottles and an environmentally safe soap. Since its introduction in late 1992, it has become a close second in market share of the scouring-pad market, not far behind Clorox Company's S.O.S. pad, the market leader.

In another example of leveraging, 3M started marketing a film for laptop computer screens based on the film it first developed in the mid-1980s for decorative signs on buildings. This thin plastic film built into screens improves brightness and conserves energy, thereby extending the battery life of laptops.

Like 3M, Hewlett-Packard has been effective at strategic leveraging of its core capabilities. It recently combined its expertise in computers with its knowledge of patient-monitoring systems to create a physician's workstation. Although still in the field-testing stage, it could greatly enlarge H-P's medical equipment business.

Hewlett-Packard also strives to use its key abilities in new and different ways. Since plain-paper fax machines use many of the same mechanisms as ink-jet printers, H-P has targeted this as one of its top candidates for product market growth. By using existing technology, H-P expects to be able to develop these faxes at no more cost than those using thermal paper.

Strategic Leveraging at 3M (continued)

The ink-jet printers are also competing against H-P's well-known laser printers. According to CEO Lewis Platt, this proactive self-destruction is necessary: "We have to be willing to cannibalize what we're doing today in order to ensure our leadership in the future. It's counter to human nature, but you have to kill your business while it is still working."

Source: Adapted from Kevin Kelly, "The Drought Is Over at 3M," *Business Week* (November 7, 1994): 140–141; and Alan Deutschman, "How H-P Continues to Grow and Grow," *Fortune* (May 2, 1994): 90–100.

Cooke found that its Dole brand connoted more than pineapple and used the brand name to launch Dole Fruit & Juice bars. These types of extensions can have definite benefits, but they require some strategic thinking and planning.

Flanker brands are used when a company wants to enter a slightly different market segment (e.g., the "cost-conscious segment") but does not want to dilute its current image. Flanker brands allow a company to retain its current position with existing customers, while still expanding into different segments. Marriott has used flanker brands to extend its position. Fairfield Inn is a low-price, low-frills product of the Marriott chain. Oldsmobile was forced to rethink the value of its brand identity when it introduced the Aurora. After a significant corporate debate, Olds decided to take its "rocket" logo (a traditional Oldsmobile symbol) off the car—at least for now—and replace it with a silver script A to attract younger buyers.[4]

The riskiest approach is to create a new product for a new market, especially if the product is not just new to the company but also new to the world. Unless the new market can be reached through existing distribution channels and/or the product can build on core competencies, this is a questionable endeavor. The company must carefully assess whether the risk is worth the effort, whether it will be possible to

The Power of Line Extensions

Extending a franchise offers a number of benefits that traditional new-product development does not. The major one is that extension capitalizes on the company's most important assets—its brand names. Thus, the company moves into a new category from a position of strength. A further benefit is that investment outlays typically necessary to establish a new brand—a significant expense—are minimal. However, line extensions must offer *new value* to customers. Companies that are successful at line extensions tend to regularly rotate the brand assignments of their product managers to prevent them from getting stuck in ruts. This reduces the likelihood of proliferating virtually identical products.

A consumer is exposed to hundreds of brand names every day. Being a well-known brand is not sufficient to be a good brand extension. Few consumers want JELL-O® shoelaces or Tide® frozen entrees. A brand can be successfully extended to a new category when it has both *fit* and *leverage*.

- *Fit* is when the consumer accepts the new product as logical and would expect it from the brand.
- *Leverage* is when the consumer, by simply knowing the brand, can think of important ways that they perceive the new brand extension would be better than competing products in the category.

Since a brand's meaning can change over time as brand extensions are introduced, management needs to develop a *brand plan*—what extensions are introduced short term and what others become possible long term. Note the changing possibilities Ocean Spray faced as they moved from cranberries to cranberry juice, to being a full-line bottled juice supplier. One must develop a long-term scenario to avoid diluting important elements of the brand and to improve the odds of pursuing more remote areas where the brand could have leverage.

Source: Adapted from Edward M. Tauber, "Brand Leverage: Strategy for Growth in a Cost-Control World," *Journal of Advertising Research* (August/September 1988): 28; and Eileen Roche, "Product Development: Why Line Extensions Often Backfire," *Harvard Business Review* (March/April 1999): 19–21.

develop and protect a competitive edge in the future, and even whether the idea is best left for the competition.

Checklist: Preparing for Strategic Product Planning

✓ Challenge yourself to (at least occasionally) lead the market and create products before customers ask for them.

✓ Strive to build a portfolio of core capabilities rather than simply a portfolio of products.

✓ Understand the reasons for your past successes and failures in new-product development.

✓ Work with engineers to understand and possibly implement a platform strategy for strategic product planning.

✓ Don't underestimate the need to come up with new-product ideas. It's risky to assume that the new-product ideas you now have are the best you can come up with.

✓ Talk to other product managers, other divisions, and other units in your company to assess whether there are some capabilities you can leverage within your product area.

✓ If brands are crucial in your industry, create a vision for the future growth and development of the brand identity or brand equity.

10

New Products: Proposal, Development, and Launch

COMPANIES HAVE INCREASINGLY found that to be successful in new-product development, it is not enough to find out what customers want and create products for those wants. They must also be able to do it better than the competition by exploiting their core abilities. In addition, there must be clarity about the company's internal process of new-product development. The Medical Products Group of Hewlett-Packard, for example, uncovered fourteen critical internal processes that differentiated successful and unsuccessful products.

> When executives at Hewlett-Packard's Medical Products Group studied 10 of their new-product failures along with 10 of their successes, they were surprised to identify a total of 14 essential tasks that determined which products worked and which didn't. The steps covered a wide range of corporate skills. Among them: figuring out which new products play to a company's core strengths, understanding how a new product should be sold, and getting an early fix on a project's costs.[1]

Product development involves many functions within a company, not just the product manager. But because product managers are frequently charged with the ultimate success of a new product, it is important to discuss their involvement in the process. Although new-product development goes beyond the fiscal year planning horizon of the marketing plan for a product line, certain portions will need to be addressed

Polaroid: Changes in New-Product Development

Polaroid, with 1993 sales of $2.2 billion, has been floundering in the new-product development front. Largely a niche player in the photography marketplace, the company's over-focus on its core abilities to the exclusion of related abilities (such as microprocessor technology) has left it unable to match the innovations that created Polaroid.

To begin attacking the problem, the company put together a benchmarking team to study how other companies handled product development. Their key recommendations were very similar to those endorsed by experts in the field. First, the company must adopt a good *process* of product development that works for the company. As Michael Hammer says in *Reengineering the Corporation: A Manifesto for Business Revolution*, "It is not products but the processes that create products that bring companies long-term success. Good products don't make winners; winners make good products." On a related note, there has to be a strategy that encompasses both the current product line and potential new entrants. Next, focus should be placed on platforms rather than individual products. This is especially critical in the high-technology fields. Finally, core abilities should be leveraged when expanding into new markets.

Polaroid's Helios 810 Laser Imaging System, a new medical imager using a chemical-free digital process, was one of the first projects to benefit from the new-product regimen. The company established a cross-functional team early in the process to both share internal ideas and obtain customer input up front. On the basis of the input, Polaroid decided to create a product that would produce pictures that could be used with the ultrasound and would be in a format familiar to radiologists. The price point, throughput, speed, and other parameters were identified and frozen as early as possible. Beta testing was conducted in the form of a year of clinical trials in hospitals.

Tackling the launch was another problem. While the product leverages the company's dry-processing technology, it is moving into a new and unfamiliar market. "These are very much relationship-selling, long-

Polaroid: Changes in New-Product (continued)

sales-cycle products. It's very different from traditional Polaroid products, so there was a lot of learning and effort into how we should bring this to a customer," says Roy Miller, director of new business development for Polaroid's High Resolution Imaging Organization. Consequently, the launch documentation and process required significant care and cross-functional cooperation.

Although it's too soon to tell whether the Helios 810 Laser Imaging System will be a commercial success for Polaroid, they've still benefited from a defined new-product development process, increased emphasis on customer contact, and the establishment of a system that will be useful for future endeavors at Polaroid.

Source: Adapted from Sharen Kindel, "Grape Expectations," *Sales & Marketing Management* (January 1995): 89–93.

each year. For some years, researching and submitting product proposals will be the extent of new-product efforts. At other times during the development project, milestones should be written into the annual plan. And, finally, as commercialization draws near, launch documentation will need to be developed and integrated into the annual plan.

Product innovation and speed of development are becoming increasingly important in our global economy. Although the role of the product manager in new-product development will vary by company, the product manager at minimum should take care in understanding and articulating the market potential and in participating on the product development team. Figures 10.1 and 10.2 examine the steps in the development process, along with the potential role of the product manager.

Note that the first step of the new-product-development process is idea generation. Ideas are fleshed out into a proposal and presented to top management (or a new-product review committee comprised of key executives of all the functional areas) for screening. For major

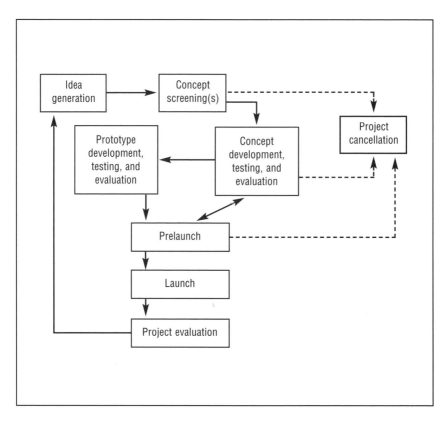

Figure 10.1 New-Product Development Flow Chart

product ideas/concepts that pass screening, management assigns representatives from relevant functional areas to a multifunctional project team for this particular new-product endeavor. The team members select a leader (who might or might not be the product manager) to organize and monitor the project, guiding it through the critical path schedule developed by the team. All members do as many tasks as possible in parallel to shorten the product development cycle. For example, product managers can conduct focus groups on concept evaluation at the same time that engineering is conducting technical feasibility studies. The dotted line from the concept development and evaluation box to the project cancellation box indicates that concepts testing poorly should be considered for elimination as early as possible rather than investing more resources in their development.

Stage	Description	Result/Output
Idea generation	Creation and databasing of ideas	New-product proposal
Screening	Examination of ideas along preestablished criteria	Assignment of project team
Concept development, testing, and evaluation	Refinement of product concept, estimation of customer interest, augmentation of business analysis (financials), go-/no-go decision	Detailed product, market, financial, and project plans; preliminary product specifications
Prototype development, testing, and evaluation	Physical development of product in R & D; functional and customer testing of the actual product (beta testing)	Final changes to product specifications and production plan
Prelaunch	Development of launch strategy; if necessary, market test or simulated market test; initial sales	Finalization of launch document; completion of product training, product support plans, sales collateral, and related written communications
Launch	Introduction and marketing of product as detailed in the launch strategy document	New-product launch
Project evaluation	Comparison of results to initial objectives	Suggested improvements for future projects

Figure 10.2 Stages of New-Product Development

During the concept development, testing, and evaluation phase, the team attempts to freeze a product's desired benefits (or preliminary specifications) by collecting marketing research information, conducting quality function deployment (QFD), and/or developing engineering drawings. At the completion of this phase, the team should obtain approval from the new-product review committee for any capital expenditures required to build the prototype.

The prototype development, testing, and evaluation phase starts with the creation of a working model or preliminary version of the product. This model is then put through use tests either inside the company's facility or by customers. Alpha tests refer to having the product used by employees or a department in the company. For example, a food item might be tested in the firm's cafeteria before testing outside the company. Beta tests refer to having a select group of customers using the product under actual usage conditions. This phase could uncover potential defects that necessitate product elimination or redesign, or it may proceed to prelaunch scale-up and production planning. It's worth noting that although prototype development is presented after concept testing and development in this chapter, the reverse order is also possible. There are circumstances in which customers cannot assess a concept in the abstract, such as when evaluating the taste of a new food product. In these situations, a prototype is required early in the process.

The prelaunch phase is the period of final preparation for commercialization. Product managers pull together details for the marketing plan, and engineering and production complete final product drawings and tool debugging. During the launch phase, the product is taken to the market, possibly through a planned roll-out. After launch, the new-product project is evaluated with a goal to either take immediate corrective action or to improve the process for the future. Each of these stages is described in the following section, from the perspective of a typical product manager.

Idea Generation

Although ideas can come from a variety of sources, both internal and external, the product manager should actively be looking for new-product concepts. Do not believe that there are already too many ideas. It is not just the number of ideas but also their quality that is important. The product manager is best suited to determine whether a flanker product is necessary to offset a competitive entry, or if a group of customers has adapted a product to a unique application that can be extended to other market segments. Subscribe to technological clipping services (either published or on-line) to monitor new developments and capabilities. Make customer visits to uncover different ways of thinking about the product category. Attend technology-sharing meetings (either within the company or through trade associations). Keep communication open with salespeople to identify opportunities. Monitor shifts in market size or composition that could suggest changing needs.

If there is no repository for product ideas in the company, create a database of ideas related to the product. Even ideas that didn't pass screening now may turn into winners in the future. Skim the database on a regular basis (perhaps quarterly or semiannually) to determine whether any ideas should be dusted off and reexamined. (Refer to Chapter 9 for more information on idea generation.)

The output of idea generation will be a new-product proposal to be examined by the individual or group of individuals who determine whether to pursue new products. The new-product proposal will have the following components:

1. **Executive Summary**: A brief synopsis of the idea and proposed plan.

2. **Present Situation**: The "fit" of the product into the strategic plan and a list of the problems and opportunities that triggered the concept.

3. **Product Description**: The specific user benefits and advantages of the product along with how the product fits in the company's total offering, with photos, illustrations, or other techniques to make the concept more tangible.

4. **Market Analysis**: An assessment of current and future market(s) for the product, competitive conditions and positioning, and any regulatory concerns.

5. **Product Development Plan**: Any resources or technology required for the proposed product.

6. **Marketing Plan**: The objectives and strategies for each area of marketing, including pricing, distribution, advertising, sales, and product support.

7. **Financial Analyses**: Projected cash flows and income statements and anticipated funds required.

8. **Supporting documents**: Marketing research summaries or any other material that supports the project.

Screening

The second step of the product-development process is screening. In this stage, the product idea should be examined according to screening criteria established by appropriate company managers, including perhaps marketing, manufacturing, R & D, and senior management. Criteria might include the following:

- Fit within existing product mix
- Patentability
- Risk of competitive entry
- Ability to sell through existing distribution
- Compatibility with strategic plan
- Acceptable payback period
- Growth potential
- Cost of tooling and machinery
- Compatibility with core technologies

The criteria for a specific company could include all or none of these factors. However, the act of listing them forces the issues to the surface and provides a forum for discussion of product concepts. The criteria should be developed separate from, and in advance of, screening particular ideas. The ideas that pass screening are prioritized, with project teams assigned as appropriate.

Many different approaches can be used for this screening process. Some companies simply indicate "must have" criteria for new products to be considered. Others list several criteria that can be evaluated on a yes-no basis. Still others use criteria with weights and ratings as shown in Figure 10.3. In this example, the most important screening criterion was "compatibility with strategic plan" as designed by the weight of 0.20. The committee rated this particular idea 0.7 for "compatibility with strategic plan," yielding a rating of 0.20 ¥ 0.70 = 0.01 (rounded from 0.014). Each row is calculated this way, then added together to arrive at the weighted rating. Note that the product idea being evaluated obtained a weighted score of 0.44. If several other ideas being evaluated simultaneously obtained scores of 0.56, 0.62, and 0.70, the relative

Requirements for a Successful New Product	Relative Weight	Rating of Product Idea											
	(A)	0.0	0.1	0.2	0.3	0.4	0.5	0.6	0.7	0.8	0.9	1.0	Rating
Fit with existing product mix	.15					×							.06
Patentability	.05				×								.02
Low risk of competitive entry	.10							×					.07
Ability to sell through existing channels	.10								×				.08
Compatibility with strategic plan	.20							×					.01
Acceptable payback period	.10									×			.09
Growth potential	.10					×							.05
Low cost of tooling and machinery	.05		×										.01
Compatibility with core technologies	.15				×								.05
Weighted Score													.44

Figure 10.3 Product-Screening Checklist

priorities would become clear. The real value of these priorities is the ability to decide how to best allocate developmental resources.

A mathematical rating device such as that shown in Figure 10.3 does not necessarily quantify results because the evaluations are still subjective. However, a screening checklist provides the opportunity for individual members to evaluate new-product ideas according to consistent parameters prior to meeting together as a group. It also fosters discussion within the new-product-development review committee and focuses the conversation on aspects considered important to the company.

Whatever type of screening tool is used, it is important that it allow a reasonable balance between being too strict and too loose. A too-strict approach can cause potential winners to be killed. A too-loose approach results in mediocre products being pursued.

After the concept passes screening, a cross-functional team is established to work on the product. The team is usually comprised of the product manager and counterparts from operations, design, and, in some cases, procurement, legal, finance, customer service, and sales. The role of the salesperson will vary by company. Although sales input and up-front support are critical, not all salespeople can identify with the top 10 percent of potential or targeted customers that represent leading trends. A recent study by AT&T comparing salespeople's judgments with customers' judgments about an innovative new-product concept found that the sales force was "consistently more optimistic and exhibited different preference patterns."[2] In that case, it may be more beneficial soliciting input from a variety of salespeople than in having sales as a core member of the team throughout the process.

Concept Development, Testing, and Evaluation

The third step of the process is concept development, testing, and evaluation. It is an extension of screening, whereby good ideas are refined and elaborated to assess their financial, marketing, and technological feasibility. The process is progressive, starting out with secondary data and in-depth interviews with a small group of customers, and then building to larger samples for more reliable estimates of market acceptance. Here the product manager is heavily involved in determining the appropriate features and attributes to maximize customer satisfaction and in estimating sales potential and profitability.

Concept development involves fleshing out the rough idea into a detailed product concept and expanding on the market size and attractiveness as presented in the initial proposal. Start with secondary data. Conduct on-line searches to get more information on market characteristics, trends, and competition. Look for any purchasable marketing research studies that have been conducted on the market. If relevant, conduct patent searches to ferret out potential future competitors. Talk with industry experts and potential customers to assess attitudes toward the product idea.

Next, solicit input from key customers who are knowledgeable and cooperative. These customers don't have to be representative, but they do have to be willing to suggest improvements and modifications to the initial concept. Probe for specific modifications that could affect the sales potential of the product. What if certain features were enlarged? Minimized? What if the product was harder? Softer? What if the dimensions were more standardized? More customized? Is color important? How about location? Get as much input from these key informants as possible.

In some cases, this type of qualitative research with a small sample is sufficient to develop the concept. In other cases, a larger sample is required to fully understand needs. When the Oldsmobile Aurora was being developed, the project team used focus groups extensively even before the first designs were drawn. In fact, more than 4,200 consumers were interviewed nationwide—the largest such sampling in GM's history.[3]

Once the concept is more fully developed, it is important to test it among a large group of customers. This group will be more representative of the target market. There is no one best approach to concept testing, but most are variations of qualitative research and focus-group discussions. Generally, several versions of a concept (possibly including competitors or placebo concepts) or several different product concepts that address the same need (i.e., substitutes) are explored in one concept test. This is because people usually provide better information when comparing alternatives, and the resulting information is more reliable than absolute evaluation. Mock ads, product descriptions on cards, drawings of the concept, and rough prototypes can all be used as part of the research. In some cases, the product's technical documentation and owner's manual is part of this analysis.

Some of the questions to be addressed during the concept test include the following: Does the proposed concept make sense to the customers? Is it preferred over what is currently available? How much value do the improvements have over existing alternatives available to the customer? Is the product consistent with the way customers currently perform the function, or will it require a change in mind-set? Would they be willing to pay more? What are the flaws? Are there changes that would make the product viable (or more viable)? What is the basic need that this product would satisfy? Has the brand name or trademark been included in the concept test?

The concept tests usually include some indication of intent to buy at some specified price. "Intent to buy" refers to the respondents' indication of the probability they would buy the product if it existed, usually expressed along a scale (e.g., 1 = "definitely would not buy" to 5 = "definitely would buy"). This is an important component of the concept test but should not be projected literally as the actual sales potential. Customers will almost always overestimate their willingness to buy in an artificial setting such as a focus group. Obtaining pricing information is difficult at best. However, determining a target price is critical for establishing a target cost for the product-development process. Although no research method is infallible, there are a few techniques that are worth trying.

One approach is to ask customers to supply a price range: What is the highest price you'd pay, above which you'd feel you were being gouged? What is the lowest price you'd pay, below which you'd question the quality of the product? Another approach is to split the concept test groups into experimental and control groups. Give each group a different price for the same described concept and determine whether there are differences in the willingness to buy at the stated prices. A third strategy is to ask customers what value (in monetary terms) the new product would have over what they are currently using. A final approach is to ask customers what they would be willing to pay for the product and what features they would be willing to give up to attain that price. In each case, an intent-to-buy question should be included.

At this point, the product team should attempt to establish a target price. The target price is necessary to estimate target costs for the developmental process. "Design by price" is an approach used by several companies in industries with rapidly changing technologies, short life cycles, and pressure on pricing.

The target price depends on the value perceived by the market. Determining value will be different for low-unit-value, frequently purchased items (e.g., consumer packaged goods) than for high-priced, infrequently purchased goods (e.g., capital equipment). The purchase of consumer packaged goods has an element of habit and inertia in the decision process. Higher-priced products may have groups or committees involved in the process. The differences in decision making, as well as the different decision makers, need to be included in the analysis.

By this time, the team should be able to list and display all the potential product features in a concept development table similar to Figure 10.4. The figure shows an example of a bicycle frame. The first column lists the needs as identified through customer and lead-user

1 Needs	2 Importance	3 Initial Metrics	4 Competitor A	5 Competitor B	6 Revised Metrics
lightweight		total mass in kg.			
can withstand rain and water contamination		time in spray chamber without water entry			
safe in a crash		bending strength of materials			
easy to install		average time to assemble			
works with a variety of attachments		list of attachments and sizes			
competitively priced		target cost range			

Adapted from Kent Ulrich and Steven Eppinger. Product Design and Development (New York: McGraw-Hill, 1995) 54–65.

Figure 10.4 Example Concept Development Table

research. Note that the needs *are what the customer wants to get out of using the product* (the benefits) rather than *how* it is to be developed. The second column contains the ranking or rating of importance of the identified needs. The third column converts the benefits into targets or goals for the designers to use in developing the frame. For example, the desired mass in kilograms provides direction (i.e., a goal) without specifying materials or production techniques. Also, the target cost range is determined by starting with the target price(s) and deducting an acceptable margin. Columns 4 and 5 list the metrics for the major competitive products. By comparing the initial and competitive metrics with the importance ratings supplied by the market, adjustments may need to be made in column 6. The final revised metrics are the output of the concept development and testing phase. Since this point represents a milestone in the new-product-development process, there should be a sign-off of the initial review committee to

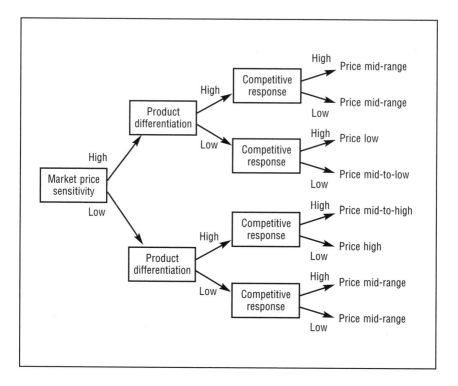

Figure 10.5 Considerations in New-Product Pricing

indicate their acceptance of the metrics, in effect freezing the *benefit set* (although actual *product specifications* won't be frozen until after prototype development).

It can be difficult completing the concept development table for breakthrough products. Customers (whether consumers or industrial buyers) do not have competitive products to use as their benchmark price. Therefore, the analysis has to start with the function being provided by the product. How is that function being done now without the benefit of the new product or service? What benefits and costs are related to changing the way it is done now? Then, both the rational and emotional motives for switching to the new product have to be considered and valued.

To estimate a target price, several things need to be considered, specifically the possibility of competitive attack, the price sensitivity of the market, and the degree of competitive differentiation. Figure 10.5 shows a tree diagram with the considerations in new-product pricing. For example, if the target customers are not price sensitive, the prod-

	Year 0	Year 1	Year 2	Year 3	Year 4	Year 5
Revenue	0	10,700	13,843	17,689	25,428	29,242
Less cost of goods sold	0	3,583	4,635	5,923	8,515	9,792
Gross margin	0	7,117	9,208	11,766	16,913	19,450
Development costs	-3,150	0	0	0	0	0
Marketing costs	0	7,200	5,814	7,430	10,679	12,281
Allocated overhead	0	1,070	1,384	1,764	2,543	2,924
Gross contribution	-3,150	-1,153	2,010	2,572	3,691	4,245
Supplementary contribution	0	0	0	0	0	0
Net contribution	-3,150	-1,153	2,010	2,572	3,691	4,245
Discounted contribution (15%)	-3,150	-1,003	1,520	1,691	2,111	2,110
Cumulative discounted cash flow	-3,150	-4,153	-2,633	-942	1,169	3,279

Figure 10.6 Projected Financial Analysis

uct is highly differentiated, and competitive response is not expected, it is conceivable to charge a relatively high price. On the other hand, if the price sensitivity is high, product differentiation low, and competition heavy, a low price will be necessary.

The appropriate technical people should be involved in the concept testing to assess the technological feasibility of any suggestions that customers might make. The concepts that appear to have marketing, technical, and financial feasibility are then subjected to a more detailed business analysis.

A rough business analysis will have been prepared prior to the idea screening (for the new-product proposal), and it will have been refined concurrently with the concept testing. It should be continually evaluated and made more definitive as new information becomes available. At minimum, it should be updated whenever a significant milestone has been reached. The skeleton proposal presented at the beginning of the process can now have some of the gaps filled in. The product description should now be more detailed, with marketing and cost objectives included. The market analysis should have more specifics on potential segments and niches, customer applications and key customer identification, and competitive benchmarks. The product-development plan should include the composition of the project team, product specifications, a critical path chart with key milestones and target dates, and implementation schedules. The marketing plan should specify planned roll-outs, short-term and long-term resource requirements, identified risk factors, and suggestions for minimizing risk. The financial analyses should be expanded to include more detailed income statement and cash-flow information than was available at the proposal stage. Figure 10.6 shows a simplified projected financial analysis for a hypothetical industrial product.

The revenue line is based on the market analysis and resulting forecast. The cost of goods sold is obtained from technical and manufacturing personnel on the product development team. The accuracy depends not only on their best assessment of per-unit costs, but also on the precision of the product manager's forecasts. The difference between the revenue and cost of goods sold is the gross margin available to cover fixed costs and contribute to profits.

The development costs include any costs already incurred for R & D and concept testing, as well as anticipated costs for prototype development, equipment and materials, labor, product testing, and additional marketing research. If the roll-out requires additional capital expenditures, they should be included here as well.

The marketing costs start at the prelaunch. These would include advertising, distribution, sales force coverage, sales promotion, and any miscellaneous selling and communication costs.

Allocated overhead refers to administrative costs allocated to various products. Some companies will assess a lower (or even no) overhead cost to new products until they have established themselves, while other companies believe that all products should provide an equal (or greater) contribution to fixed costs (i.e., a type of "hurdle"). Regardless of the company's attitude toward cost allocation, it is imperative that the estimated revenue (either price or number of units) is not artificially inflated simply to cover these costs.

The gross contribution is the amount of revenue remaining after development costs, marketing costs, and overhead costs are subtracted from gross margin. This is the amount of money that the product is expected to contribute to indirect fixed costs of the firm and taxes and profit.

The supplementary contribution is used when new products have an effect (positive or negative) on existing products. The resulting cash flows should be included on this line and either added to or subtracted from the gross contribution to arrive at the net contribution. In Figure 10.6, gross contribution and net contribution were the same because the new product was not expected to have any impact on existing product sales.

The discounted contribution line shows the net present value of each net contribution figure, discounted at 15 percent per year. The last line shows the cumulative cash flows over time.

Before progressing to prototype development, it is important to revisit the questions that were used to evaluate the initial project and verify that it is still an attractive endeavor. If the new information gathered results in the project no longer passing the initial screening questions, the new product may need to be modified or cancelled. This can be a critical milestone when another go/no-go decision must be made.

Prototype Development

If the proposed product passes the concept test and evaluation, it moves into R & D and/or engineering to be developed into a physical product. Up until now it existed only as a verbal description or a rough mock-up. Now it must be translated into a technologically feasible product. This does not mean that marketing (or product management) is no longer involved. Rather, the product manager's job is to ensure that the core benefits that were the essence of the product concept are not lost during the development process and that progress is being made on the marketing plan, trade-name search, and other factors critical to new-product success. That is why a project team approach is so crucial.

After the prototypes have been developed, they should be put to rigorous functional and customer testing. The functional tests are conducted under both laboratory and field conditions to be sure the products are safe and reliable (i.e., consistently perform as they are designed to perform). Customer tests are conducted to be sure that the design is appropriate. Market testing, in-home testing, and beta testing are all variations of the types of tests to be performed at this stage.

> Some manufacturers have built gigantic mechanical gizmos that can replicate almost any kind of abuse a product encounters. For example, a car takes a trip through Chrysler's huge climate-controlled lab where robotic drivers subject it to scorching heat and ice storms. Gerber recruits future customers of both sexes at birth and, with the help of

enthusiastic parents, maintains a test panel of 2,500 toddlers through age three.

In order to make its PowerBooks even more customer-proof, Apple Computer puts all new models through common indignities. These include drenching them in Pepsi and other sodas, smearing them with mayonnaise, and, to simulate conditions in a car trunk, baking them in ovens at temperatures of 140 degrees or more.[4]

The selection of appropriate beta sites can have an impact on launch success for several reasons. First, the companies or individuals selected should have sufficient knowledge to thoroughly test the product and identify any potential problems or improvements. Second, they should have "reference value" to use as success stories at the time of launch. Third, they should have good relations with the salesperson in the territory as well as with the company to be able to withstand the risk of product failure without long-term damage.

Some questions to be answered during this stage are as follows: Does the prototype work as intended? Does it meet specs? Does it satisfy customer needs? Are there any anticipated production problems? Can they be overcome within a reasonable time and cost? Has production scheduling been finalized? Is it on schedule? Have costs been confirmed? Have raw materials been ordered? Is marketing ready for launch? Are there minor modifications that can improve the product or its value without adversely impacting the project? Is there a need for a significant change that will necessitate a delay in the project?

If all these questions can be answered positively, the product specifications should be frozen and the screening committee (i.e., top functional positions) should sign off to indicate their acceptance of the specifications. Then, the project is ready to move to the next stage: the prelaunch.

Prelaunch

The prelaunch is the period prior to commercialization when the product manager verifies that all preparations have been made for the actual product introduction. During this stage, the product manager must identify all stakeholders and determine their information requirements. Customer service needs to be prepared to handle inquiries and fulfill orders. Technical support personnel may require specialized training.

The distribution channel may require advance warning of any unique requirements of the product or service.

Also at this time, there may be a need to consider a market test or a simulated market test to determine whether the strategy (not just the product) is ready for introduction. Various use tests already should have determined the viability of the product, but the tests might not have addressed the best way to go to market. Test marketing helps assess whether the right price is being charged, whether the appropriate message is being communicated through advertising, and whether the proper distribution strategy is being employed. Of course, test marketing is expensive in terms of both money and time. Therefore, it should be undertaken only when the risk of not doing it is great.

For a typical test market, the product manager selects a geographic area that is as representative of the product's target market as possible and markets the product on a limited basis in that region. The key decisions to be made include how many test markets, which ones, and how long the tests should run. Most companies select two or three test markets that provide good representation of their target customers. Good representation refers to assuring that critical demographic variables are dispersed in the target area in about the same proportion as exists in the total market area. The length of the test market will vary depending on the type of product. Some will require six to nine months, and others will need two years. The factor to consider is the length of the buying cycle, with the test market being at least as long as two buying cycles.[5]

Based on this information, a launch plan can be developed. The launch documentation should contain three specific components: (1) a milestone activities chart, (2) the marketing strategy to support the launch, and (3) an early indicator chart. (See Figure 10.7.) All of these guide the launch and early commercialization.

The milestone activities chart lists the desired dates of completion for significant activities such as purchasing equipment for the launch, finalizing package design, obtaining legal clearance, subcontracting specialized labor, and preparing the owner's manual. Each of these may require several steps and may vary in importance depending on the project. Their potential impact on product success must be considered in assessing priority. For example, electronic or high-tech consumer products require clarity in technical documentation to be successful. Customers are

Figure 10.7 Components of a Launch Control Document

increasingly seeking simplicity in a complicated world. However, as a recent *Business Week* article stated, "Plain English is a language unknown in most of the manuals that are supposed to help us use electronic products."[6] The format of the milestone activities chart can vary from a simple list of activities and dates to more formal project schedule and control techniques like Gantt and PERT charts. (Refer to operations management or project management books for more details.)

The marketing strategy component of the launch materials details the tactical components of the launch. Branding, packaging, pricing, advertising, and all aspects of marketing are studied. As with the annual product plan, the new-product marketing plan should start with an objective such as "Convert 25 percent of current customers to the product upgrade and obtain trial by an additional 25 percent." The marketing tactics would then be put into place to accomplish this objective. A sample outline for this new-product marketing strategy is shown as Figure 10.8. Some companies include all or most of the listed components; others will need to be more selective. Line extensions might require only an abbreviated outline, whereas breakthrough products will need extensive marketing strategy plans.

As mentioned earlier in the chapter, a decision will need to be made whether to price a product high initially to recover the development costs or to price it low to gain market share faster. Now you have more

A. New-product objectives

1. Sales volume
2. Market penetration

B. Background summary

1. Total industry sales volume and trends
2. Major competitors and analysis
3. Market potential and segments
4. Corporate charter

C. The company's new product/service

1. Product specifications/description
2. Brand name, trade name, and/or trademark
3. Why is your product better?
4. Main user benefits
5. Customer profile(s)
6. Primary selling points
7. Positioning
8. Potential barriers
9. Frequency of purchase/use

D. Entry strategy

1. Timing: when should the launch be planned?
2. Roll-out sequence: what are the priority markets?
3. Publicity

E. Company support/preparation

1. Internal announcements
2. Sales force tools
3. Customer service training
4. Technical support training
5. Field seminars
6. Policy statements

F. Marketing plan

1. Product marketing objectives
2. Target markets
   - New or existing customers
   - Demographics; psychographics
3. Distribution
   - Channels (including Internet)
   - Mark-ups/commissions/other incentives
   - Available selling tools
4. Pricing
   - Base price and discount schedule
   - Promotional pricing programs
   - Option pricing
   - Product-line pricing
5. Promotion
   - Sampling
   - Merchandising
   - Customer training
6. Advertising
   - Product announcements
   - Press releases
   - Trade shows
   - User groups
   - Direct mail
   - Advertising (media and copy strategy)

G. Cost and schedules

1. Development of sales support
2. Training costs (including lodging and travel)
3. Trade shows
4. Media and advertising costs
5. Sampling and merchandising costs
6. Calendar of training schedules
7. Media calendar
8. Event schedule

Figure 10.8 The Supporting New-Product Marketing Plan

information than was available early in the process and you are able to fine-tune the pricing. A number of factors affect this decision. First, how likely is it that competitors will enter the market soon? The ability of competitors to enter the market will be based on the investment required to enter, the ease of entering, and their own strategies. The faster that competition is likely to enter, the more appropriate a penetration (low) price strategy. Second, is there a large enough segment of customers willing to pay a high price for the product initially? Third, is the company, product, or service positioned appropriately for the price strategy being considered? Finally, what are the payback period, "hurdle rates," and return required by the company?

The final component of the launch documentation (after completing the milestone activities chart and the various event calendars and schedules from the marketing plan) is a calendar of early indicators of potential launch success. Early indicators refer to outcomes, such as the number of inquiries, that can help predict or provide early indicators of the level of launch success. For example, history might indicate that thirty inquiries typically convert to one sale. In that case, tracking the number of inquiries could provide an early indicator of future sales. Other early indicators might include the number of sales calls made on the new product, the percentage of distributors willing to carry it, the awareness level of the market, the number of facings retailers give to the product, and so on. After identifying the early indicators, the next step is to set time-based (e.g., weekly, monthly) goals to achieve for each. The early indicator chart, then, lists the outcomes expected by the end of designated time periods (e.g., each month), enabling the product manager to compare actual against expected performance without waiting for final sales data.

With launch documentation prepared, the product is ready to move to the launch phase. It's worth noting that sales training may sometimes be required during the prelaunch phase (perhaps six to nine months prior to the official launch). The information on sales training is presented in the next section covering the launch stage.

Launch

The next step of the new-product-development process, launch, results in the introduction of the product into the market. Decisions need to be made about timing (when to launch the product), geographic strategy, target market prospects, sales and customer service support, and final marketing strategy.

Timing can be a critical component of new-product success. If competitors might be (or are) entering the market, the product manager must decide whether to get there first, concurrently, or after the competition. First entry usually provides an advantage, but if rushing results in a flawed product, the result can be more damaging than good. Timing an entry with competition can neutralize the competitor's potential first-mover advantage as well as possibly increase the potential market faster. Delaying an entry until after competition is in the market might make it possible to capitalize on competitive flaws as well as benefit from any competitive advertising that educates the market. Timing is also important if there are seasonal or cyclical aspects to a product, or if the introduction impacts the sales of existing products.

It is also necessary to make decisions on a geographic strategy. On some occasions, a national launch is appropriate, but most new products start with a roll-out strategy. Prioritize the markets (e.g., regions, industries, or countries) and decide on an entry sequence. For example, it might be desirable to first enter the most attractive markets in terms of size and dollar potential. Or it might be more desirable to enter markets where competition is weak, providing an ability to gain experience, exposure, and market position. In other situations, the selection of roll-out markets is based on different product applications, pipeline inventory in the markets, ability to gain distributor or retailer support, company reputation in the market, or a host of other factors.

Although the roll-out might appear similar to test marketing, it differs in a couple of important ways. First, in a test market the product manager targets regions that are representative of the final launch. This is not the case with a roll-out. The markets are selected based on their ability to provide an early cash flow or to gain commitment from an influential market needed for the continued roll-out. Second, the test market is a final test before the commercialization decision is made. The roll-out is the first step in commercialization after the decision is made.[7]

As part of this geographic strategy, identify specific target market prospects. This is particularly important in the business-to-business market where clients/prospects can be listed by name. The more detail that can be provided here for the sales force, the greater the chances of encouraging them to sell the new product. That leads right into sales support. Work closely with the sales force to provide them with information that will help them sell. Prepare "how to sell it" booklets that discuss customers (not target markets), applications (not features), and useful questions to ask on a sales call. Make sure that customer service stays in the loop with sufficient communication through internal newsletters, informal and formal meetings, and various announcements.

The last part is fine-tuning of the introductory marketing strategy. This action plan details introductory pricing, base price, and option pricing; press releases and product announcements; direct mail to select customers; shipping policies and procedures; channel and end-user communications; and training for the sales force and/or customers. The sales training in particular should help salespeople *sell* the product rather than simply *pitch* the product. (See Figures 10.9 and 10.10).

The sales training that is part of the product launch should educate and motivate the salespeople to sell your product. In other words, why

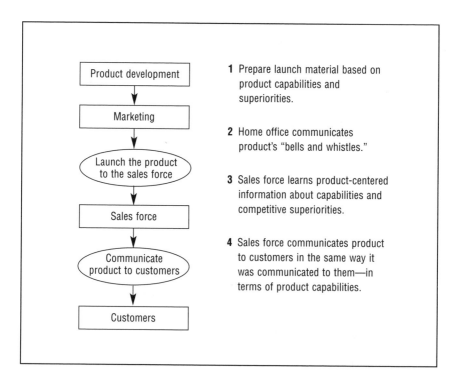

Figure 10.9 Avoid the "Pitch-the-Product" Launch

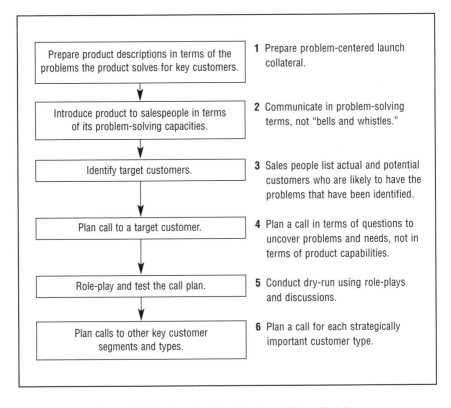

Figure 10.10 Provide Need-Centered Sales Training
in the Product Launch

should the salespeople believe the product will perform as claimed? What motivation is there for them to sell it? For an existing product, the best proof is past sales success. For new products, a bit more persuasion is necessary. Results from test marketing or beta testing, statements from sales managers or other salespeople indicating their success in a roll-out region, sales that you (as product manager) have personally made, or trade shows and lead generation programs in place can convince salespeople that the product is worth their time and effort to pursue. In addition, financial and nonfinancial motivators should be considered. Higher commissions, better bonuses, and desirable contests can work under the right circumstances. (See feature Launching a New Product to a New Customer Segment: The Catera.) Nonfinancial motivators could include customer input suggesting that less sales effort is necessary to be successful, the ability to sell the product along with another product with a minimal increase in selling time, or unquestionable proof of competitive superiority.

A portion of the training might also include a motivational explanation of the need for and use of market intelligence by product managers, and how providing this information can help the salespeople. A standard intelligence report form can be built into a call report, designed into the menu system on a computer, or included as part of the expense form. Because this information typically comes into sales management or sales administration, a process would need to be established to send a copy of relevant product-related data to the appropriate product manager. The type of information useful for submission might include the following:

- New-product announcements by competitors
- Effective and ineffective approaches to selling a product
- Changes in competitive strategies
- Unusual product applications by customers, especially if they indicate a trend
- Perspectives on market trends that might affect company strategy

Project Evaluation

After (or during) the launch stage, some type of project appraisal should be completed. The main objectives of this stage are to improve future product development efforts and to move the product from a new-product status to being an ongoing product requiring long-term maintenance. There may also be a need on occasion to relaunch a product that is not meeting expectations. The relaunch should be considered as early as possible, and hopefully will have been uncovered by the early indicators as discussed in the prelaunch section of this chapter. If the product is still an acceptable product, changes to the marketing strategy may need to be made to make it a success. (See feature Relaunching the Advanced Photo System Cameras: Fuji.)

Launching a New Product to a New Customer Segment: The Catera

When Cadillac introduced the Catera (an entry-level luxury car), it had to shift from its existing market of older, loyal customers and appeal to a demographic segment unfamiliar to its dealers. To inspire dealerships to get behind this new product, it created Catera College. The college consisted of two-and-a-half days of sessions providing information about the new customer base and the vehicle itself. At the college, dealers drove the car and saw it taken apart piece by piece. For dealers who could not attend, Cadillac rented out theaters across the country. On the big screen, dealers were presented with an up-close look at their customers, as well as the teamwork involved in selling the product. While the training itself was not an incentive to sell the product, it provided the tools necessary to make the incentives (such as a contest) work, and both were tied to Cadillac's Standards for Excellence (SFE) awards.

> Dealerships were awarded points for success in such categories as technician training, salesperson training, and customer service. Every month, each dealership receives its standing in the contest. The grand prize is a trip to an exotic locale with a twist. Just sending winners to the beach to drink cocktails and watch the sun set is not part of Cadillac's game plan. The company has made intensive business seminars a major focus of the trip. [In 1997] when the Catera was being launched, the grand prize was a trip to Germany to see the Catera built.
>
> SFE winners appreciate the dual purpose of the trip. "There are meetings in the morning to discuss ways to better your dealership. The goal is to get you to look at your store and find ways to improve it," says Ed Nimnicht, president and CEO of Nimnicht Cadillac in Jacksonville, Florida. "Then you get some leisure time to enjoy winning the contest."

Part of the product launch incorporated tests for dealers. They earned points for answering questions properly and had to demonstrate a minimum knowledge level to get into the program. In addition, selling the Catera was a requirement for dealers trying to win Cadillac's "Master Dealer Status."

Source: Condensed from Kenneth Hein, "Preparing for the Launch," *Incentive* (April 1997): 45–49.

Relaunching the Advanced Photo System Cameras: Fuji

Years of research and development through a consortium consisting of Canon, Eastman Kodak, Minolta, Nikon, and Fuji spawned the Advanced Photo System (APS). APS is an innovative 24-millimeter camera system promising clearer, sharper photographs than possible with traditional 35-millimeter point-and-shoot equipment. Based on an agreement to protect the five companies against charges of collusion, the companies were banned from informing retailers and consumers about APS cameras and film until February 1, 1996. There was also a common shipping date of April 15 so that all five companies would have the same marketing start dates. The stringent secrecy rules curtailed much of the research that would normally have gone into a product launch, as Fuji learned.

> Almost to the day the system was launched, information about it was kept from the trade press, photo retailers, consumers, and even from most Fuji employees. This prevented the company from conducting valuable market research—information that would have accurately forecasted retailer demand for the product and enabled the company to create more effective advertising campaigns.
>
> Generally, new Fuji products are "sold" to the sales force at least six months before the launch date. But the secrecy surrounding APS prompted the company to hold off on sales training for several extra months . . . . Three months before the February 1996 launch, Fuji sales managers in each territory attended an intensive training session. Bill Homer, Fuji's vice president of U.S. field sales, says that training focused on the history, features, and benefits of APS. Although the session also included a discussion of "the benefits and potential of the system" Homer adds that it was "very intensive from a hardware standpoint."

The APS system was officially launched February 1996 at the Photographic Marketing Association (PMA) annual trade show. All the players had underforecast and were unable to meet retailer demand. Therefore, they had to pull ads, and by the second half of 1996 promotions for the system all but died out. In 1997, Fuji and Kodak relaunched their products based on the common technology.

Relaunching the Advanced Photo System Cameras: Fuji (continued)

Fuji polished its positioning and education techniques with the help of increased marketing research. For one thing, it discovered its advertising had been off the mark. The company had tried to present too much information to consumers rather than presenting one or two primary benefits. It changed the advertising to key in on selected benefits; then placed a new commercial in a time slot during the Seinfeld series finale in 1998. It also stepped up education for retailers and consumers. Fuji equipped its sales force with training videos and flip charts and helped them teach dealers how to sell the system. And finally, it strengthened relationships with mass-merchant retailers.

APS cameras captured 20 percent of the point-and-shoot camera market by early 1999, with an expectation of doubling that number by the end of 1999. This was aided by Fuji's relaunch—a launch based on effective communication with the sales force, with supply-chain partners, and with customers.

Source: Condensed from Tricia Campbell, "Back in Focus," *Sales and Marketing Management* (February 1999): 56–61.

Checklist: Keys to Successful New-Product Development

✓ Know the market and what it needs.

✓ Select new products that play to a company's core strengths.

✓ Create a multifunctional project team early in the process.

✓ Get an early fix on costs and price.

✓ Get quality and price right the first time, even if it means delaying the launch.

✓ Freeze the product concept (i.e., obtain commitment on what benefits it will provide the customer) after the concept development stage.

✓ Freeze the product specifications after successful prototype development.

✓ Build checkpoints into the system to make sure the developing product still meets the initial criteria under which it was approved.

✓ Do not introduce a new product simply to meet a new-product goal; be sure it fits the corporate strategy and customer requirements.

✓ Conduct alpha, beta, or market tests to gather user input.

✓ Include milestone activities and early warning indicators, along with relevant dates, in the launch control plan.

✓ Design a roll-out strategy to incrementally reach the best markets for the new product.

Case Three[1]

The Many Aspects of Product-Line Management

PRODUCT-LINE MANAGEMENT involves conceiving and developing new products, but also extending existing product lines and building brand equity. Different companies emphasize different parts of these product line management activities, and a given product manager will emphasize different aspects, depending on specific needs at the time. Examples of each are presented below in this case study.

Developing New Products

In developing new products, product managers use a variety of techniques to reduce risk and increase chances of success. First, product managers (particularly in highly technical fields) have learned to begin next-generation products immediately after the launch of prior-generation products. Intel started this approach in 1990. Second, developing simultaneous products based on a corporate strategy leverages the success of both products by adding momentum. Intel demonstrated this as well with its ProShare family of products. Third, generating several products from a common platform spreads out development costs and allows products to be brought to market more quickly and at a lower price. Hewlett-Packard benefited from this knowledge in the introduction of its color Deskjet printer. Finally, establishing barriers to entry for the competition affords at least a temporary competitive edge. Here again, Hewlett-Packard discovered this in its work in inkjet printers.

Intel's Next-Generation Products

Companies are finding it necessary to bring out more products faster, particularly in high-tech fields. Intel, for example, has been picking up the pace of product development in the face of competition. It used to develop microprocessors sequentially, bringing them out about four years apart, as shown in Figure 10.11.

	286	386	486	Pentium	P6	P7
Start of design	1978	1982	1986	1989	1990	1993
Introduction	1982	1985	1989	1993	1995	1997 or 1998

Figure 10.11 Intel's Product Introduction Schedule

The sixth- and seventh-generation chips, on the other hand, were in process long before prior versions were introduced, with an emphasis on new applications and strategic alliances. Note that both the P6 and P7 were already under development when the Pentium was introduced. The P6 is focused on new applications, such as voice recognition and videoconferencing. The P7 is being designed under a new architecture with Hewlett-Packard. In 1994, an agreement was signed to meld Intel's traditional data-processing methods with H-P's reduced instruction set computing (RISC) technology.

To enhance the future launch of the P6 chip, as well as increase market potential for the Pentium, Intel developed and rolled out a new family of desktop videoconferencing products for PCs. This new family of products will enable computer users to work on the same document simultaneously over regular phone lines. The new-development activities are consistent with Intel's vision of bridging the gap between communications and computer industries, as Tim Clark explains in the *Business Marketing* article "Intel Sets $8 Million Campaign":

> Intel is positioning the new line as convergence products. "Along with our many partners, we are facilitating the convergence of the communications and computer industries, turning the personal computer into a personal conferencing tool," [said] CEO Andrew S. Grove.

Working on simultaneous product platforms along with mutually beneficial product entries, as Intel has done, represents a couple of techniques companies have used to improve their product development processes. They've demonstrated the need to be proactive and plan strategically for new-product development, as has Hewlett-Packard.

Hewlett-Packard's Inkjet Printers

In an effort to maintain its dominance in printers, Hewlett-Packard has beaten Japanese competitors by using their own tactics. Over a decade ago Japanese companies had taken away the lead in hand-held calculators, a market H-P had pioneered. The success was due to a mass-market strategy with low-priced, well-designed products. This time, H-P took that approach with inkjet printers, as Stephen Kreider Yoder explains in "How H-P Used Tactics of the Japanese to Beat Them at Their Game" in *The Wall Street Journal*:

> H-P engineers adopted two Japanese tactics: They filed a blizzard of patents to protect their design and frustrate rivals, and embarked on a process of continual improvement to solve the inkjet's problems. They developed print heads that could spit 300 dots an inch and made inks that would stay liquid in the cartridge but dry instantly on plain paper. One engineer tested all types of paper: bonded, construction, toilet, and, for good measure, tested sandpaper, tortillas, and socks.

Hewlett-Packard established a solid foothold in the black-and-white inkjet printer market using these techniques. However, it faced another challenge in 1990. At this time, H-P engineers were working on a color printer, intent on bringing out a full-featured, mechanical marvel. Marketing suggested they build on the platform they had already established, since they felt this approach, though less sophisticated, would satisfy the needs of the customers:

> There was a near mutiny among the engineers until a product manager named Judy Thorpe forced them to do telephone polls of customers. It turned out people were eager for the product the engineers considered a "kludge." H-P learned that "you can tweak your not-so-latest thing and get the latest thing," Ms. Thorpe says. By sticking to the existing platform, H-P was able to get the jump on competitors in the now-booming color-printer market.

One other thing: H-P's "blizzard of patents" set up a barrier to entry for competition. Competing engineers lost valuable time negotiating H-P's maze of fifty patents covering how ink travels through the head. By the time Canon became a serious competitor, H-P had sold millions of printers and had practiced continual improvement in manufacturing. Later, when Canon introduced a color inkjet in 1993, H-P was able to cut the price of its version before Canon even reached the market. As a result, Hewlett-Packard "owns" 55 percent of the world market for inkjets. And, like Intel, H-P is leveraging its knowledge of inkjets in other areas such as fax machines.

Extending Existing Product Lines: Successes and Failures

Sometimes products are not completely new, but rather they are product-line extensions. As a product manager plans for line extensions, there must be a careful balance between variety and redundancy. Fast-moving consumer goods are perhaps particularly vulnerable to this trap. In an effort to respond to competitive entries, to reach smaller market segments, to bolster short-term gain, and/or to gain more shelf space, many product managers offer too many variations of core products.

Numerous examples of extending product lines abound. When Nabisco introduced its line of Fat-Free Fruit Bars in 1993, the cookie category was growing at a modest 2 percent per year. Nevertheless, this line of offerings resulted in Nabisco's sales increasing three times as fast as the overall market. Similarly, when 7-Up introduced Cherry 7-Up in 1987, the new product variant was successful, and the sales of the core product also went up.

Unfortunately there are pitfalls to line extensions. Introducing a product variation under the same name as a core brand could have the potential of weakening the brand equity. Line extensions can generally be easily matched by competitors. A number of hidden costs can arise due to increased production complexity, more errors in forecasting, and the loss of consumers due to potential out-of-stock situations.

As an example, John Quelch and David Kenny, in the *Harvard Business Review* ("Extend Profits, Not Product Lines") discuss the plight of a U.S. snack foods company they refer to as Snackco. Over time, Snackco's product line had grown, but its overall sales remained flat. In evaluating the situation, the company studied the effectiveness of core products, niche products, seasonal and holiday products, and filler products. The percent of the line as well as the percent of the sales volume accounted for by each type of product are shown in Figure 10.12.

	Percent of Line	Percent of Sales Volume
Core products	20%	70%
Niche products	10	10
Seasonal and holiday products	5	10
Filler products	65	10

Figure 10.12 Snackco's Product-Line Analysis

By looking at this analysis, it was clear changes had to be made. Note that the core products generally followed the Pareto principle: 20 percent of the products accounted for 70 percent (instead of Pareto's 80 percent) of the volume. These were also the key products responsible for building company and brand reputation. Consequently, Snackco managers changed manufacturing and delivery schedules to assure that core products were always in stock.

The niche products were holding their own, contributing 10 percent of the product line and 10 percent of the volume. These products were studied to determine in which market areas they had sufficient volume to continue, and in which markets they should be dropped.

Seasonal and holiday items provided 10 percent of the sales volume even though they represented only 5 percent of the product line. These items were maintained with additional store displays provided for active selling periods.

Finally, filler products were evaluated. Even though the per-unit contribution was greater than for some of the other products, it wasn't enough to offset the fact that with 65 percent of the product line they were contributing only 10 percent of the sales volume. These products were carefully evaluated in terms of true costs and competitive need. The company decided to cut the number of filler products. The greatest cuts were in competitive areas where the company decided to use the shelf space to build share in core products. In leadership markets, the cuts were more selective with a goal of blocking shelf space from the competition.

Note the steps that Snackco took to perform this analysis. First, the *sales/profit/contribution history* of each of the items in the product line was collected and analyzed, along with data on customers and competitors. Part of this was based on internal records. But to be able to fully *evaluate product performance*, external research was also required. Random store checks indicated that the most popular items were out of stock up to 50 percent of the time and that up to 40 percent of customers bought either a competitive product or nothing. The remaining customers purchased one of the filler products. The company also used consumer tracking panels to gain data on both household purchases and usage frequency.

After examining this information, Snackco managers were challenged *to add value to existing products and to the product line*, particularly for retail channel members. As Quelch and Kenny point out, they had to be able to prove that retailers would benefit from the product-line plan being proposed:

> Snackco's managers believed that the new strategy was on target, but they also knew that without the support of the sales force any efforts to implement the plan would fail. So, backed by Snackco's president, one of the sales regions undertook a four-month test to determine the impact of refocusing core products versus continuing line extensions. Not only did market share increase during the test, but sales-force compensation also increased because of the faster turnover of the more popular items in the line, which were given additional shelf space at the expense of the slower-moving items.

To *boost market penetration*, usage rate and/or the number of users had to be increased. Some of this was accomplished by scheduling manufacturing and delivery to assure that core products were always in stock, as well as providing additional store displays for the seasonal products. However, some advertising changes were also necessary:

> Snackco shifted from an umbrella advertising approach for the whole line to a strategy that focused on its flagship products. Advertisements for these products emphasized the Snackco brand and thereby promoted the brand's line extensions. Over the past two years, Snackco has made significant gains in market share and volume, which in turn have generated even higher margins.

11

The Financial Side of Product Management

PRODUCT MANAGERS NEED to establish a framework of financial plans, budgets and controls related to their products, services, and customers to be able to make sound decisions. The starting point is a foundation of financial and managerial accounting to better understand the profit contribution of their offerings so that decisions on product rationalization, pricing, and product-line management can be made. From a broader financial perspective, product managers should understand key ratios and concepts drawn from an understanding of financial statements.

General Cost Classifications

In manufactured product environments, there are two major cost classifications, manufacturing and nonmanufacturing, each of which has subclassifications. *Manufacturing costs* include all those related to the transformation of raw materials into final products, including direct materials, direct labor, and manufacturing overhead.

- *Direct materials,* such as wood in tables and steel in cars, become an integral part of the finished product and can be considered direct costs. Other materials, such as glue, may be more difficult to link to individual units of production and may be classified as indirect materials to be included in overhead.

- *Direct labor* includes the labor directly traceable to the creation of products. Research and development, support-staff time, and other labor not directly related to manufacturing are included in indirect labor.
- *Manufacturing overhead* includes all costs of manufacturing, excluding the direct material and direct labor costs described above. Included in this category are items such as indirect material, indirect labor, heat, light, and depreciation.

Nonmanufacturing costs include the marketing, sales, administrative, and support costs unrelated to the production of products. These are typically included on the SG & A (selling, general, and administrative) expenses line of an income statement. Historically, the non-manufacturing costs have been less significant than the manufacturing costs for most products. However, the growth of services and the emergence of various technologies have reversed the relative weight of these costs in many companies.

- *Marketing and selling costs* include advertising, shipping, sales commission, and salaries.
- *Administrative expenses* include executive, organizational, and clerical salaries.

Both manufacturing and nonmanufacturing costs result from the normal operation of a business. In addition, there may be other expenses, such as the purchase of an asset, that are charged to the income statement for the period, even though they are not operating expenses. These costs are presented in the simplified income statement on the next page. The cost of goods sold includes the direct material and labor as well as manufacturing overhead. The data are frequently derived from *standard* costs and are a combination of fixed and variable expenses. (Standard costs are predetermined cost amounts that represent what cost *should* be under the most efficient methods of operation; in other words, they are benchmarks for measuring performance.) Similarly, the overhead expenses (comprised of the nonmanufacturing or SG & A expenses) may be a combination of fixed and variable costs.

The income statement resulting from the above process of listing costs provides a historical review of the results of operations. It does

```
                    Sales
                         − cost of goods sold
                    Gross Profit
                         − operating expenses
                    Net Income from Operations
                         + other income
                         − other expenses
                    Net Income Before Taxes
                         − income taxes
                    Net Income
```

Figure 11.1 Simplified Income Statement

not necessarily provide the information for planning and improving the decision-making process of product management. To provide this type of information, it is necessary to distinguish between the variable and incremental costs associated with products to better understand their contributions to overhead and profit.

Concepts of Segmented Reporting

Variable costs are those that vary in direct relation to the activity level. If activity level doubles, variable costs double in total. This is true because the cost per unit stays approximately constant over a relevant range of activity. Direct materials and direct labor are variable production costs, and sales commissions represent a variable sales expense. In addition, there may be step-variable (similar to incremental or semifixed) costs. Setup time, seasonal labor, and similar activities related to the amount of business can be considered variable to that piece of business. *Fixed costs*, on the other hand, do not change regardless of changes in the level of activity. Since fixed costs remain constant in total, the amount of cost per unit goes down as the number of units increases. It is sometimes said that variable costs are the costs of *doing* business, whereas fixed costs are the costs of *being in* business.

Once costs have been separated into fixed and variable elements, it is easier for product managers to determine the contribution of different products or customer segments. It is also easier for companies to evaluate the performance of several product managers. A comparison of a traditional income statement (using historical cost information) and a contribution income statement (separating fixed and variable costs) is shown in Figure 11.2.

Note that in Figure 11.2 the top line (sales revenue) and the bottom line (net income) are the same using both approaches. However, using the contribution margin approach it becomes clear that these particular sales contribute $9,300 to fixed costs (prior to break-even) and profit (after break-even is achieved). (See Chapter 12 for a discussion of break-even analysis as it is applied to pricing decisions.) This concept of contribution reporting can be applied to business units, departments, product managers, product lines, customers, or similar units of analysis. When applied to these segments, direct costs and common costs must be understood.

Direct costs are those that can be identified directly with a particular unit of analysis (i.e., product manager, product, customer, etc.) and

Traditional			Contribution			
Sales	$17,000		Sales		$17,000	
less cost of goods sold	11,000		less variable expenses			
			var. production	$5,000		
			var. administrative	$2,200		
			var. selling	$500	$7,700	
					$ 9,300	
Gross margin			Contribution margin			
less operating expenses	$6,000		less fixed expenses			
administrative	$2,000		fixed production	$4,000		
selling	$3,000	$5,000	fixed admin.	$1,500		
			fixed selling	$2,800	$8,300	
Net income before taxes		$1,000	Net income before taxes		$1,000	

Figure 11.2 Traditional Income Statement Versus Contribution Income Statement

that arise either because of the unit or because of the activity within it. *Common costs* are those that cannot be identified directly with any particular unit, but rather are identified in common with all units. The common costs (most likely fixed costs) cannot be allocated except through arbitrary means. An example of contribution reporting is shown in Figure 11.3. Note that this example presents an income statement constructed for the product managers as if they were businesses. In this example, company revenues are $900,000, of which $500,000 come from Product Manager 1 and $400,000 come from Product Manager 2. They contribute $80,000 and $170,000, respectively, with $160,000 in overhead not allocated to either. The $400,000 revenue of Product Manager 2 comes from a standard model ($150,000) and a custom model ($250,000) contributing $70,000 and $140,000, respectively. Product Manager 2 has $40,000 of fixed expenses not related directly to either product. The custom product receives $180,000 from contractors and $70,000 from residential customers to generate its $250,000 in revenue. The segment contributions are shown without an arbitrary allocation of the $10,000 of fixed costs for the custom model which aren't directly related to either customer group.

Cost Drivers

Before a product manager can price a product or evaluate a product line, he or she must understand what the cost drivers are for the various products and customers. Some customers require additional expediting charges, others require special shipping and handling, while others expect free services. Each of these costs should be allocated to the particular product or customer to determine the true financial contribution.

Financial Statement Analysis

As suggested earlier, financial statements are historical documents indicating what happened during a particular period of time. This perspective helps a product manager judge past performance through the use of ratios. In addition, by comparing changes in the statements over

Units of Contribution Analysis

	Total Company	Product Manager 1	Product Manager 2
Sales	$900,000	$500,000	$400,000
Less variable expenses			
cost of goods sold	400,000	270,000	130,000
other variable expenses	100,000	70,000	30,000
Total variable expenses	500,000	340,000	160,000
Contribution margin	400,000	160,000	240,000
less direct fixed expenses	150,000	80,000	70,000
Product manager margins	250,000	$80,000	$170,000
less common fixed expenses	160,000		
Net income	$90,000		

	Product Manager 2	Standard Model	Custom Model
Sales	$400,000	$150,000	$250,000
Less variable expenses			
cost of goods sold	130,000	50,000	80,000
other variable expenses	30,000	20,000	10,000
Total variable expenses	160,000	70,000	90,000
Contribution margin	240,000	80,000	160,000
less direct fixed expenses	30,000	10,000	20,000
Product margins	210,000	$70,000	$140,000
less common fixed expenses	40,000		
Net income	$170,000		

	Custom Model	Contractors	Residential
Sales	$250,000	$180,000	$70,000
Less variable expenses			
cost of goods sold	80,000	60,000	20,000
other variable expenses	10,000	3,000	7,000
Total variable expenses	90,000	63,000	27,000
Contribution margin	160,000	117,000	43,000
less direct fixed expenses	10,000	7,000	3,000
Customer segment margins	150,000	$110,000	$40,000
less common fixed expenses	10,000		
Net income	$140,000		

Figure 11.3 Contribution Reporting

time, it is possible to identify performance trends and use the information for subsequent decisions.

Investment Decisions

Directly or indirectly, product mangers may be involved in capital budgeting decisions in the preparation of investment proposals for new products, new markets, or new business ventures. The most common methods of evaluating different proposals are average rate of return, payback period, present value, and internal rate of return.

The *average rate of return* is the ratio of the average annual profits to the investment in the project. Using this method, the product manager prepares a forecast of the improvement in profit over a number of years from a given investment. The total profit is divided by the number of years to give an average annual profit, and this is then expressed either as a percentage of the original investment or as a percentage of the average investment per year. Assume the following stream of profits from, for example, a new product:

> Year 1: $100,000
> Year 2: $200,000
> Year 3: $300,000   Average: $240,000
> Year 4: $250,000
> Year 5: $350,000
> Total: $1,200,000

If the initial investment was $1 million, the average annual profit would be the $240,000 as a percent of $1 million, or 24 percent. Alternatively, the $240,000 could be expressed as a percentage of the average investment for each of the five years. In either case, the rate would be compared to hurdles used by the company or to industry norms.

The *payback period* is calculated by determining the length of time (number of years) it takes to recover an initial investment. In the above example, the investment of $1 million is paid back during the fifth year. After four years, the cumulative profits are $850,000, with the remaining $150,000 being earned sometime during the final year. Here again, the payback as an absolute value is less important than looking at the relative values of different projects.

The *present value* (or net present value) refers to the value of future cash inflows compared to the current outflow of the initial investment.

The *internal rate of return* is the interest rate that makes the present value of all projected future cash flows equal to the initial outlay for the investment. In other words, it is the rate that makes the net present value (NPV) equal zero. The calculation is somewhat complex mathematically, and since it is a value that would be provided by your financial group, the definition should be sufficient for our purposes.

Checklist: Financial Management

✓ Be sure to understand and analyze the cost drivers (e.g., expediting) behind your products and customers as part of the pricing process.

✓ Use contribution reporting to get better information for decision making. Understand the contributions by both product and customer.

✓ Gain a comfort level with income (profit and loss, or P & L) statements as well as balance sheets.

✓ Clarify the return or hurdle rate required for new-product development.

Part IV

FUNCTIONAL SKILLS

T he core product or service is only part of the "package" a customer buys. Price, brand reputation, purchase convenience, and other factors influence the success of a product.

Therefore the product manager has to be competent in dealing with these marketing support aspects of the product. Price must balance company costs and profitability with customer satisfaction. The product manager must be aware of the financial costing of the product, the impact of price concessions, typical aspects of price sensitivity, potential competitive reactions, and the need to consider channel members in pricing decisions.

Marketing communications can provide favorable or unfavorable, strong or weak, consistent or inconsistent messages to the market. Careful monitoring is required to determine the best trade-offs among various advertising vehicles, sales collateral materials, trade shows, seminars, and sales promotion techniques.

Also, the method used to go to market might need to be changed or at least refined. As distributors and retailers gain more knowledge of and influence with end-users, product managers need to cultivate them to assure product success.

Part IV highlights the marketing skills necessary for a successful product line. Special attention is devoted to pricing and marketing communication decisions and activities.

12

Pricing Products and Services

AN IMPORTANT PART of a product manager's marketing function is pricing a product to balance profitability and customer satisfaction. For existing products, the seven-step process described in this chapter provides the basic considerations for setting prices and making price changes. The seven steps involved in setting price are as follows:

1. Determine corporate strategy and the role of price.

2. Evaluate costs related to the pricing decision.

3. Estimate the price sensitivity of the target market(s).

4. Anticipate competitive actions and reactions.

5. Assess potential legal consequences (if appropriate).

6. Calculate profit implications.

7. Incorporate price changes/implementation in the product plan.

Determining Corporate Strategy

The first step, determining corporate strategy, should have been accomplished in the business assessment (Worksheet 5.1). The corporate direction might specify a premium position or a mass-merchandiser/discount approach. These obviously have direct impact on the pricing. It is necessary to know if a product is a cash cow, is being used to enter a new market, or requires a specific ROI, when setting the price. On the other hand, in a decentralized organization the corporate position might have minimal impact on product planning, and price will play a neutral role.

Avoiding price wars might be part of a corporate pricing strategy. For many companies, this can be done only by reducing the cost of producing products, as Heinz Pet Products chief Bill Johnson found out. After facing intense price pressure from the competition, Johnson decided that meeting price cuts, without also lowering the internal cost structure, would be deadly.

> "We decided to run pet foods assuming the price war would never end," he says. To do so, he turned the pricing equation on its head. "Instead of calculating out what it cost to make cat food and price accordingly, we asked ourselves what did consumers want to pay," Johnson explains. His team decided that today's finicky customers would pay between 25 cents and 33 cents per 5½-ounce can, tops. Johnson then went to work rationalizing processes to hit that target. Step one was identifying his company's competitive advantages: strong brand equity, cheap materials in the form of excess tuna from Heinz's StarKist operations—which goes into more than 15 percent of Pet Foods' products—and some proprietary manufacturing processes. "Step two," says Johnson, "was a draconian reduction of cost."[1]

Part of the corporate strategy involves positioning. Is the product positioned as the market leader, thereby commanding a premium price? Which competitors are you most directly linked with? Sometimes the price/value positioning can be affected by selection of competitive comparisons. When Woolite (a detergent for fine washables) first entered the market it positioned itself as an alternative to dry cleaning rather than a substitute for less-expensive soaps. It was consequently perceived as a better "bargain." Similarly, when the Chrysler Towne & Country introduced its new-model minivan in 1995, it positioned the various features against luxury vehicles, again modifying the competitive price. Take an active role in helping your customers determine the reference value they use in determining whether your product's price is acceptable. (See Figure 12.1.)

- Which competitors?
- High-end products in your company
- Other relevant frames of reference

Figure 12.1 Establish Reference Values to Reduce Your Customer's "Sticker Shock"

Evaluating Costs

Evaluating the costs related to the pricing decision is often more difficult than it seems. Companies use different approaches for allocating costs, so the variable and fixed costs can become blurred. Nevertheless, definitions of these common pricing terms are relevant.

Variable costs are those that vary (in total) with production of the product or service. This could include direct materials and labor. For a given production level, these are constant per unit and provide the floor for pricing decisions. Fixed costs do not vary with production or sales; they exist whether or not the product is even produced. Fixed costs can be allocated according to square feet of production space or percentage of a product's contribution to total revenue, split equally among product managers, or a variety of other approaches. In the long run, *all* costs must be covered, and the long-term pricing of products should consider all costs. However, in the short run, any price obtained that exceeds variable costs can at least contribute to fixed overhead and (potentially) profit.

Variable costs will often be equal to the cost of goods sold and be the only incremental costs relevant to a pricing decision. There are exceptions when fixed costs are incurred for a bid situation, for example, that are incremental to that decision. In that case, the incremental fixed costs must be added to the variable costs to determine the floor for pricing decisions.

	Sales
Less	Variable costs
	Contribution margin
Less	Fixed operating expenses
	Net operating income
Less	Other expenses
	Net income

Figure 12.2 Simplified Income Statement

This information should be reflected in a contribution report form of an income statement. (See Chapter 11.) A simplified income statement is shown in Figure 12.2.

Fixed costs can include the fixed costs directly attributable to a product line as well as other allocated costs. The fixed costs directly attributable to a product line would be the operating expenses for that product. Subtracting these from the contribution margin yields the operating income a product manager provides. Other allocated costs would be subtracted from this figure to arrive at net income.

The following break-even formula can be used as a starting point for evaluating a price. The standard break-even formula shows the number of units that must be sold at a given price to cover all costs. The formula is:

$$\text{Break-even units} = \frac{\text{Fixed costs}}{(\text{Price} - \text{Variable cost per unit})}$$

Therefore, if relevant fixed costs are $42,000, the product has a price of $10,000, and the variable cost per unit is $4,000, it would be necessary to generate sales of seven units to break even. By experimenting with different price levels and matching that with expected

	(1)	(2)	(3)
Revenue			
(10 @ $10,000)	$100,000		
(10 @ $9,000)		$90,000	
(12 @ $9,000)			$108,000
Cost of Sales			
(10 @ $4,000)	$40,000	40,000	
(12 @ $4,000)			$48,000
Contribution Margin	60,000	50,000	60,000
Operating Expenses	42,000	42,000	42,000
Net Operating Income	$18,000	$8,000	$18,000

Figure 12.3 Price/Profit Comparison

demand, the product manager can begin the pricing analysis. In addition, a target return (profit) can be included in the numerator (along with fixed costs) to assess the unit sales necessary to contribute a specified profit. For example, if a required profit of $12,000 were added to the fixed costs in the numerator, it would be necessary to generate sales of nine units to break even.

Building on this example, suppose a product manager of consulting services handling ten projects for $10,000 each has direct costs of $4,000 per project and overhead costs of $42,000. Each project contributes $6,000—the difference between the price and the variable costs—to overhead and profits. The operating profit would be $18,000, as shown in the first column of Figure 12.3.

But, if facing competitive pressure the product manager drops the price to $9,000 per project, each project would contribute only $5,000 to overhead and profit. Assuming no other changes, the new revenue would be $90,000, and the new bottom-line profit would be $8,000.

% break-even sales change = $\dfrac{-(\% \text{ price change})}{(\%CM + \% \text{ price change})}$

% break-even sales change = $\dfrac{-(-.10)}{.60 + (-.10)} = \dfrac{.10}{.50} = .20$

Figure 12.4 Modified Break-Even Formula for a Price Change

The 10 percent drop in price (from $10,000 to $9,000) would result in a 55 percent drop (from $18,000 to $8,000) in operating profit (see the second column in Figure 12.3).

To keep its profit at $18,000, the firm would need to land two more jobs. Because we assumed that operating expenses—fixed costs—don't change with an increase in unit sales, the objective is to provide a contribution margin of at least $60,000. Hence, the firm would need to handle twelve projects rather than ten ($60,000 divided by the new per-project contribution of $5,000), as shown in the third column of Figure 12.3. The two additional jobs represent a 20 percent increase in sales to compensate for the 10 percent drop in price.

By adapting the break-even formula presented earlier, it is possible to quickly look at the impact of a price change. The modified formula is shown in Figure 12.4. CM stands for contribution margin (the difference between price and variable cost, or $10,000 - $4,000 = $6,000, in this example). The %CM refers to the contribution margin per unit expressed as a percentage of the price ($6,000 divided by $10,000). The result is the percentage change in unit sales necessary to contribute the same profit return as now.

This formula can be used in an electronic spreadsheet (e.g., Quattro, Excel, or Lotus) to see the impact of price changes. Putting relevant contribution margins in the columns, potential price changes in the rows, and the formula in the cells yields a spreadsheet similar to Figure 12.5.

Price Change (%)	Contribution Margin								
	0.65	0.60	0.55	0.50	0.45	0.40	0.35	0.30	0.25
0.10	-0.13	-0.14	-0.15	-0.17	-0.18	-0.20	-0.22	-0.25	-0.29
0.09	-0.12	-0.13	-0.14	-0.15	-0.17	-0.18	-0.20	-0.23	-0.26
0.08	-0.11	-0.12	-0.13	-0.14	-0.15	-0.17	-0.19	-0.21	-0.24
0.07	-0.10	-0.10	-0.11	-0.12	-0.13	-0.15	-0.17	-0.19	-0.22
0.06	-0.08	-0.09	-0.10	-0.11	-0.12	-0.13	-0.15	-0.17	-0.20
0.05	-0.07	-0.08	-0.08	-0.09	-0.10	-0.11	-0.13	-0.14	-0.17
0.04	-0.06	-0.06	-0.07	-0.07	-0.08	-0.09	-0.10	-0.12	-0.14
0.03	-0.04	-0.05	-0.05	-0.06	-0.06	-0.07	-0.08	-0.09	-0.11
0.02	-0.03	-0.03	-0.04	-0.04	-0.04	-0.05	-0.05	-0.06	-0.07
0.01	-0.02	-0.02	-0.02	-0.02	-0.02	-0.02	-0.03	-0.03	-0.04
-0.01	0.02	0.02	0.02	0.02	0.02	0.03	0.03	0.03	0.04
-0.02	0.03	0.03	0.04	0.04	0.05	0.05	0.06	0.07	0.09
-0.03	0.05	0.05	0.06	0.06	0.07	0.08	0.09	0.11	0.14
-0.04	0.07	0.07	0.08	0.09	0.10	0.11	0.13	0.15	0.19
-0.05	0.08	0.09	0.10	0.11	0.13	0.14	0.17	0.20	0.25
-0.06	0.10	0.11	0.12	0.14	0.15	0.18	0.21	0.25	0.32
-0.07	0.12	0.13	0.15	0.16	0.18	0.21	0.25	0.30	0.39
-0.08	0.14	0.15	0.17	0.19	0.22	0.25	0.30	0.36	0.47
-0.09	0.16	0.18	0.20	0.22	0.25	0.29	0.35	0.43	0.56
-0.10	0.18	0.20	0.22	0.25	0.29	0.33	0.40	0.50	0.67

Figure 12.5 Spreadsheet Example of Break-Even
Analysis of Price Changes

What would have been the necessary change if the variable costs were lower (e.g., $3,500) so that the contribution margin was 65 percent, with everything else equal? In this case, it would have been necessary to increase sales by only 18 percent to break even. What if variable costs were significantly higher (e.g., $7,000) so that the contribution margin was only 30 percent? Again, with everything else the same, what sales change would be necessary to break even? Now the answer is 50 percent, or five additional projects. Price increases also can be evaluated by using Figure 12.5. However, if a price increase is necessary, it can be useful to time the increase with a product change or additional service that adds value.

So, in looking at price changes it is necessary to understand what impact those changes have on required volume to break even, and then ask a couple of questions. How much leverage do competitors have? If their variable costs on this product are lower, they would be able to withstand a price cut longer. How likely is it that they would want to cut price and sustain it? Also, how sensitive are customers to price changes? Is it possible to sell the required volume change? Remember that the information in the spreadsheet doesn't give you "the answer." Rather, it simply provides one data point to help you make a better decision.

Estimating Price Sensitivity in the Target Market

The third step is estimating the price elasticity of the target market(s). Although there are some research-based techniques for estimating price sensitivity, conducting this type of research is at best difficult. As a starting point, begin with a managerial assessment, asking the following questions:

- How strong is the product positioning, its differentiation in the customers' eyes? Is the differentiation based on an important, relevant characteristic? *(The stronger the differentiation and the more important it is perceived by the customer, the less sensitive to price the customer is likely to be.)*
- Is there a lot of competition? Are customers aware of the competition? Can customers find substitute ways of fulfilling the same need without buying any product? *(The fewer options the customer has for providing the same benefit(s) a product provides, the less sensitive to price the customer is likely to be.)*
- What was the impact on sales when there were price increases/decreases in the past? Consider both internal and competitive price changes. *(If prices were raised in the past without a significant loss to the competition, the customer is likely to be less sensitive to price.)*

- Is the product part of a larger purchase? *(The smaller the product purchase is as a percentage of a larger purchase, the less sensitive to price the customer is likely to be.)*
- Is the product a capital expenditure or an expense item? *(The less expensive the absolute price of the product, the less sensitive to price the customer is likely to be, unless a small unit-volume item is bought in such large quantity as to result in a major expenditure.)*

After completing the managerial assessment, research might be necessary to gather more specifics. Here is some of the information that would be beneficial: What are the highest and lowest prices that fall within the customer's relevant range? What does price mean to the customer? Is the absolute or comparative price more important? Are customers considering shipping and operating costs as part of the price? Part of this analysis should include a search for new products and markets where price is less important. (See feature Using Innovation to Reduce Price Competition on page 214.)

Remember that a market can be multilevel. If the product is sold to as well as through intermediaries such as distributors, dealers, and retailers, the price charged has to consider them as well. First, price so that their margins will be large enough to motivate them to do what they need to do. Second, consider how the margins they add affect the price the end-users ultimately pay. Third, corporate and pricing positions have to be consistent with image of the channel member. Finally, use the spreadsheet you created from the break-even sales equation (Figure 12.5) to begin setting the discount structure for the channel.

Part of the job of product managers is to *manage the expectations of their customers.* First of all, it's important to not *artificially raise* expectations (through advertising or sales promises) to a level that cannot consistently be attained. When true performance falls short of expected performance, customers perceive a lower level of value (and feel the price is too high). Secondly, you can help customers set *realistic* expectations by thoroughly explaining contract terms, providing benchmark data on standard product performance, or demonstrating the impact on their bottom line given price-performance data. (See Figure 12.6.)

- Don't artificially raise expectations.
- Prepare customers for future pricing issues.
- Help customers set realistic expectations.

Figure 12.6 Manage Customer Expectations

Anticipating Competitive Actions and Reactions

The fourth step in pricing requires a look at the competition. First of all, how do the prices compare with the major competitors? What benefits do the products provide that have perceived value to the customers? It is useful here to try to put a monetary value/cost on the differences between the product and its competitors. Much of the information will be subjective, but it still forces evaluation of the cost/benefit analysis more carefully. Start with the competitor's price, and then add and subtract internal estimates. (See Figure 12.7.)

Assessing Legal Consequences

The Sherman Anti-Trust and the Robinson-Patman Acts are the two pieces of legislation most relevant to pricing decisions. The Sherman Act (along with amendments of the Clayton Act) prohibits practices that reduce competition or inhibit trade. Collusion or price fixing is one such practice. Companies may not legally collude with competitors to set prices (horizontal price fixing), and they may not require channel members to charge certain prices (vertical price fixing).

The Robinson-Patman Act prohibits certain forms of price discrimination. In general, it is illegal to sell "products of like grade and qual-

Competitor's price			$5,000
Value of added benefits			
Monetary savings			
Longer life	$500		
Lower failure rate	250		
Labor savings	1,000		
Total savings	1,750		
Monetary costs			
Switch-over costs	-500		
Economic value to the customer		1,250	
(The $1,250 is a best estimate of the true "worth" of differences between the product and the competition. It should be added to the competitor's price to arrive at the economic or financial value to the customer.)			
Incentive to switch		750	500
(The $750 is the amount subtracted from the economic value to make the product more attractive and provide an incentive to switch.)			
Your price			$5,500

Figure 12.7 Estimating Monetary Value of Competitive Differences

ity" at different prices to competing resellers if the result is to restrain trade or put one reseller at a competitive disadvantage to another.

Calculating Profit Implications

The sixth step in pricing demonstrates the bottom-line impact of the prices and price changes—typically in the form of a profit and loss (P & L) or income statement. Some companies that use a cost-plus-markup approach want to see the impact of price changes on a per-unit basis. This is appropriate when there is a relatively low number of high-ticket sales. However, for most products the impact of a markup can be deceiving if forecasted sales are not taken into account. If there are

Using Innovation to Reduce Price Competition

As always, one way to exit a price war is to innovate. Take Becton Dickinson's hypodermic needles. The company produces over a billion each year, at a paltry dime apiece, worth over $100 million in sales. Prices have been flat to down over the past decade. During one particularly painful period in the late 1980s, a Japanese competitor began selling its wares for 7 cents a unit. In other words, you would not want to be stuck in the needle business. Then, Becton Dickinson got together with Baxter International, which had developed InterLink, a needleless needle.

The point to remember is that the needles doctors stick in your arm account for about 50 percent of the market. The other half are used to hook up intravenous lines to other IVs, which is where the Baxter-Becton team made its mark. InterLink looks like a regular syringe except the needle is replaced by a hard piece of tapered plastic tubing that ends in a blunt tip. Baxter created a new type of plastic-and-rubber seal that could be punctured and then would reseal around such a plastic spike. Baxter asked Becton to produce the spike.

Hospitals gladly pay more for InterLink because the pointless needles lower the risk of accidental needle sticks. [In 1993,] health care workers reported about one million sticks, costing hospitals upward of $400 per incident in lost time and paperwork, excluding any legal or long-term health costs. "That's the attraction," says Gary Cohen, a marketing VP with Becton Dickinson. "Even though InterLink needles cost about 25 cents, hospitals save money."

Source: Andrew E. Serwer, "How to Escape a Price War," *Fortune* (June 13, 1994): 90.

several products in the line or multiple price combinations for different market segments, it is useful for planning purposes to present all of this information in an impact table, perhaps using a spreadsheet format. (See Figure 12.8.)

	Product 1			Product 2			Product 3			Total
	Price A	Price B	Price C	Price A	Price B	Price C	Price A	Price B	Price C	
Sales units										
Revenue										
Cost of goods sold										
Gross margin										
Total gross margin										
Operating expenses										
Operating income										
Other expenses										
Net income										

Note: The "Total" column provides the bases for the income statement in the annual product plan.

Figure 12.8 Price Change Impact Table

Incorporating Price in the Product Plan

The last step in pricing is to incorporate pricing into the marketing plan. As mentioned earlier, the way you position your price against the competition and the tactics you use to manage customer expectations should be built into the marketing plan. It is also important to think about what makes your product different from and better than the competition. Then find ways to make these differences visible, beneficial, and believable. (See Figure 12.9.) When a mattress company wanted to visibly demonstrate how its inner coil springs operated independently from one another, it set up bowling pins and dropped a bowling ball on the bed. Since the ball was able to bounce without

- Visible
- Believable
- Beneficial

Figure 12.9 Tangibilize Areas of Differentiation

causing the pins to fall, it demonstrated the benefit of the coil springs. When car companies or tire companies want to focus on the benefits of their safety, they frequently use a baby to represent the importance of the safety feature. When companies want to convince customers of a particular fact, they will use third-party testimonials or government documentation to make it believable.

Do not forget that several internal customers (e.g., customer service, sales, other product managers) must be informed of the approved changes. Also, some pricing strategies might require additional promotional material, changes in packaging, or other things that could affect the marketing plan. If a price change is being tested in a certain region or for a certain period of time, be prepared to track the results for making future decisions.

Finally, keep track of pricing tactics used by other firms both inside and outside of your industry. Sometimes novel approaches can be adapted to unique needs. Here are a few examples to start an idea file:

- *No-haggle pricing* is offering a set price in an industry known for "negotiation." This is currently being used by Saturn and Ford Escort in the automotive industry.
- *Always the low price* is charging a constant low price rather than using frequent promotions. This is used at the retail level by Wal-Mart and at the manufacturer level by Procter & Gamble.
- *Step pricing* is a discount policy in which prices are reduced for set quantities in a step-wise fashion: for example, one

Zebra Technologies Fights Price Competition with No-Frills Product

Zebra Technologies Corp., a Vernon Hills (Ill.) maker of barcode printers, had developed a reputation among customers as a manufacturer of high-quality, top-of-the-line printers. But the company also saw a lot of sales potential in the low-end portion of the marketplace. A low-priced, low-frills printer was a cinch to make. But offering such a model posed two risks: It might tarnish Zebra's image of quality with its customers, and, worse, it might cannibalize the existing product line.

The solution? Zebra came up with a no-frills version with a plastic housing that pleased its clients. But it didn't give away the store: It made sure that the stripped-down $1,495 printer couldn't be upgraded to ensure that it wouldn't compete with its high-end $1,995 model, which is faster and can print on different kinds of materials. The result: The new Stripes printer helped Zebra's sales climb 47 percent last year, and margins on the new printer match those from Zebra's original line.

Source: David Greising, "Quality: How to Make it Pay," *Business Week* (August 8, 1994): 58.

price for 1–100 units, a reduced price for 101–300 units, a still-lower price for 301+ units, and so forth.

- *Price point pricing* is setting price points across a product line to denote quality differences. Many consumer products are priced this way, using a "good-better-best" approach in terms of quality. Structure the prices so that customers are most likely to buy the highest-profit product in the line. Sometimes it is preferable to introduce a lower-priced variation than to reduce the price of a core product. (See feature Zebra Technologies Fights Price Competition with No-Frills Product above.)

- *Peak-time pricing* is charging a higher price for peak-period usage and a lower price for nonpeak times. Phone companies, utilities, and movie theaters routinely use this approach.
- *Bundled pricing* is creating a "package" of features or products and selling the bundle for one price. Car companies use this approach with their option packages.
- *Unbundled pricing* is taking packages apart and selling components individually. Many products in the mature phase of the product life-cycle use this approach, allowing customers to select and pay for specific features only. Unfortunately, customers frequently attempt to start with the low price of a main component and negotiate inclusion of free features, reducing the effectiveness of this technique.
- *Trial pricing* is charging a low price for new products or new customers to encourage trial of a product.
- *Quantity discount pricing* is a technique that involves several variations. Companies can charge a reduced price for a given quantity per order, cumulative quantities over a fiscal year, or some combination of these options.
- *Cross-connected pricing* is allowing a discount on one product/service when purchasing another. It is commonly used among airlines, car rental firms, and hotels.
- *Leasing* is paying a time-based fee (e.g., weekly or monthly) for the right to use a product. It is used increasingly in the automotive industry as an alternative to purchasing the vehicle.

Checklist: Pricing Products and Services

✓ Forget everything you know about how pricing is done in your business. The best new ideas you can get are from outside your industry.

✓ Avoid raising or lowering prices simply in response to competition or internal costs. Assess how your customers might respond to the change and determine whether this reaction justifies the change.

✓ Consider a no-frills product variation as an alternative to price cutting when faced with competitive pressure.

✓ Time your price increases with added value.

✓ Understand the contribution margins of all products in your line, and the impact that has on pricing decisions.

✓ Conduct a managerial assessment of how sensitive your target market is.

✓ Innovate and look for new product-market segments where price sensitivity is lower (and your product will be able to obtain a higher price).

✓ Anticipate competitive reactions before making price changes.

13

The Product Manager as Marketing Manager

MARKETING ENCOMPASSES A multitude of activities involved in getting a product to the right market at the right time and at the right price. Since the product manager is ultimately responsible for this, it is critical that marketing services (e.g., advertising, marketing research) and distribution strategy not be ignored. Making sure that the right competitive position is established is the starting point for the development of an effective strategy.

How is the product/service different from the competition? This can be a tricky question, particularly for commodity products like mortgages. However, Arbor National Mortgage, a midsize company in Uniondale, New York, has developed a positioning approach that has worked. By repackaging a standard mortgage into a bridal registry, the result was a distinctive identity.

> Arbor takes a standard Fannie Mae mortgage and repackages it into the Arbor Home Bridal Registry. Couples register with Arbor instead of a department store so friends and families can contribute to the newlyweds' first home. "Running the registry is a lot of work, so we aren't as concerned with getting couples to register as we are in getting inquiries about purchasing a first home," says Boyles [Arbor's senior vice president of marketing]. "Only three dozen couples have actually registered, but we've had over 5,000 couples call about the service. Their names are now in our database. We hope to have them

as customers someday." Arbor also holds mortgage seminars for real estate brokers, accountants, and consumers. And the company plants a tree for customers who want one, either in their yard or in a public forest.[1]

Product managers shepherd this process through a variety of functional areas and are responsible for communicating the appropriate messages to the target market(s), setting a price consistent with the value provided and evaluating the distribution activities to ensure superior end-customer satisfaction. Chapter 12 examined pricing considerations. This chapter looks at the advertising, distribution, and various support components of the marketing function.

Marketing Communications (Marcom) Planning

The marketing communications (marcom) portion of the product plan addresses the setting of the advertising objectives, media planning, and creative strategy. In some cases, publicity, telesales, and/or sales support will be part of the plan. This is the direction of "integrated marketing," tapping into the potential synergy of all communication vehicles. Product managers are usually more interested in direct-response activities than in purely image or corporate advertising. Even consumer marketers are becoming increasingly involved in database marketing, with the aim of targeting messages more effectively and measuring the response to the investment in advertising.

Setting Objectives

The starting point for the advertising plan is the setting of objectives. The statement of objectives would follow the same format as the overall marketing objective. It would include what to communicate to whom and with what results. Should the advertising generate sales, produce leads, or enhance an image? To whom must the message be communicated to make that happen? What will be the result of this communication? $X revenue? Number of leads per prospects reached? A percentage change in awareness? If the product manager runs a mail-order operation with no sales force, it might be appropriate to have an objective of generating $X sales from a defined target market over the next twelve months. But most companies would have some combination of sales, lead generation, and/or image reinforcement.

If the product is not sold directly to the end-user, a decision must be made about what part of the budget will be devoted to advertising to the end-customer (a pull strategy) and what part will be devoted to trade advertising (a push strategy). These two groups will require different media and different messages.

After deciding what to communicate to whom and with what results, the next question is how to make it happen. That is the essence of the advertising plan: deciding on the media and creative strategy. Although much of the detail work will be handled by the company's advertising department or through an advertising agency, the product manager needs to understand the basics to make good evaluative decisions. The media planning will consist of (1) listing potential media, (2) selecting appropriate media vehicles, (3) assessing trade-offs, (4) examining media combinations, and (5) developing a media calendar. The creative strategy converts the positioning and unique selling features into effective customer communications.

Media Planning

Media planning starts with selecting the appropriate media and media vehicles to accomplish the stated objectives. Decide how many to use (to increase reach) and how often to advertise in each (to increase frequency). Then coordinate resources to get maximum return from the investment in advertising. That means it is sometimes necessary to violate traditional turf boundaries that separate the media (including boundaries between marketing and sales) and focus on the intended results (objectives) of the advertising.

List Potential Media   Start by developing a list of all media and promotional methods that could be used to accomplish the objectives. Analyze each according to editorial format, circulation, frequency, and cost. Then prioritize the list according to each medium's ability to contribute to the plan's effectiveness. The larger the potential audience, the more a product manager will need to consider broad-reach media. The smaller the audience, the more targeted the media must be.

Database Marketing

A growing number of marketers are investing millions of dollars to build databases that enable them to figure out who their customers are and what it takes to secure their loyalty. In 1992, for example, General Motors Corporation joined with MasterCard to offer the GM Card. As a result, GM now has a database of 12 million GM cardholders, and it surveys them to learn what they're driving, when they next plan to buy a car or truck, and what kind of vehicle they would like. Then, if a cardholder expresses an interest in, say, sport-utility vehicles, the card unit mails out information on its truck line and passes the cardholder's name along to the appropriate division.

Blockbuster Entertainment Corporation is using its database of 36 million daily transactions to help its video-rental customers select movies and steer them to other Blockbuster subsidiaries. In Richmond, Virginia, the company is testing a computerized system that recommends ten movie titles based on customer's prior rentals. The suggestions are printed on a card that also offers targeted promotions. Customers who have rented children's films, for example, might get a discount at Discovery Zone, Blockbuster's playcenter subsidiary.

Source: Adapted from Jonathan Berry, John Verity, Kathleen Kerwin, and Gail DeGeorge, "Database Marketing," *Business Week* (September 5, 1994): 57.

The primary media choices for consumer communications are listed in Figure 13.1. It is not a comprehensive list but is simply intended to trigger a few ideas for thinking through the media options. The primary media choices for a business target market include some of the consumer media choices but go beyond as well. (See Figure 13.2.)

Select Appropriate Vehicles   Second, select the most appropriate media vehicles. A message of quality is best carried in a publication that is a "bible" of the industry, whereas announcements of new industrial prod-

Category	Some "Best" Uses	Rate/Cost Considerations
Print *Newspapers*	• Ads that don't require high print quality • Local coverage of all demographic segments • Inserts • Coupons	• Agate line or column inch rates • ROP (run of paper) • Color rates • Insert rates
Magazines	• Demographic selectivity • Color print quality	• Page rates (or fractions of) • Color rates • Bleed rates • Cover rates
Broadcast *Radio*	• High frequency • Auditory messages • Appeal to specific demographics	• Daypart (e.g., drive time) • ROS (run of station) • Local, spot, network
Television	• Mass coverage • Impact of sight and sound • Short message (except for infomercials)	• Daypart (e.g., prime time) • Specific programs • Local, spot, network
Direct mail	• Direct response • Identified audience • Long message	• List rental • Postage rates
Publicity	• "Newsworthy" events • Credibility	• Personnel/time costs
Miscellaneous *Outdoor*	• Frequency • Mass local audience	• Poster size • Traffic count
Transit	• Frequency	• Inside/outside/station posters
Point-of-purchase	• Stimulate impulse buying	• Retailer negotiation
Internet	• Interactivity • Two-way communication	• Start-up and maintenance costs

Figure 13.1 Consumer Media Considerations

Category	Some "Best" Uses	Rate/Cost Considerations
Print		
Newspapers	• Frequency (compared to trades) • For select markets where news-papers are significant	• Agate line or column inch • ROP (run of paper) • Preferred position • Color rates (if available)
Trade journals	• Product appeals to specific reader profile • Product can benefit from image of journal	• Page rate (or fraction of) • Color rates • Preferred position
General business publications	• Need to reach a broad mix of influencers or decision makers	• Same as above
Consumer publications	• No trade reaches your market • You can afford the additional impressions even at the expense of wasted coverage	• Same as above
Directories	• Purchasing agents play a role in the sale	• Ad size
Card decks	• Low-cost products	• Number of inserts
Broadcast		
Television	• Large target market • Corporate or image advertising	• Selected programs
Radio	• Primary market concentrated in limited geographic areas • Frequency	• Daypart • ROS (run of station) • Local, spot, network
Direct Mail	• Identified audience • Lead generation or direct sale	• List rental • Postage rates
Sales literature/ brochures	• To advance the sales call	• Print charges
Catalog	• Reference material	• Print charges

Figure 13.2 Business Media Considerations

Trade shows	• Demonstration of product	• Booth charges • Direct and indirect labor
Publicity	• "Newsworthy" events	• Direct and indirect labor
Internet	• Interactivity • Two-way communication	• Start-up and maintenance costs

Figure 13.2 Business Media Considerations (continued)

ucts are better placed in new-product digests. For product managers not working through an agency (either internal or external), some preliminary information on the media vehicles can be obtained from Standard Rate & Data Service directories available at libraries with business collections. From that information, the product manager can estimate the cost per prospect for each media vehicle. After narrowing the list, request media kits from the rest to obtain more specific information on reader profiles, frequency discounts, ability to obtain reduced list rental with a paid ad, and information about the effectiveness of advertising in the specific publication or broadcast medium.

Assess Trade-offs Third, assess the trade-offs between the size (cost) of the ad, the impact on prospects, and the number of times it can be placed. The cost of a large ad is more than the cost of a smaller ad. However, because a large ad is seen (noted) by more people, the cost per person noting the ad can provide more efficiency. The assessment should also include placement within the medium. For magazines, ads on the covers, front part of the publication, adjacent to specific editorial content, and/or isolated from other advertisements usually have the most effectiveness. For radio, drive-time spots typically reach more people than ROS (run of schedule). For television, news has the greatest audience size, although specific programs might have a closer match to the target audience. For direct mail, odd-sized and dimensional mailings can have more impact, but they increase the cost, thereby limiting the potential reach and frequency of the mailings. In general, with a given budget, it is usually better to increase frequency at the expense of reach rather than to increase reach at the expense of frequency.

What is the necessary frequency of communication to maximize response? That depends on several things. Messages promoting a unique product or having a unique format require less frequency to be noticed than "commodity" ads. The more advertising messages a person is exposed to at one time (e.g., within one publication), the greater the number of insertions required to break through the clutter. The more complicated the message or the less differentiated, the more likely it is that more than one impression will be required to be effective.

Examine Media Combinations   Fourth, examine combinations of media that could increase effectiveness. This is the "synergy" part of integrated marketing. For example, timing a telemarketing sales call right after the intended receipt of a direct mail piece can increase the response. Using different media simultaneously can sometimes break through the target market's perceptual barriers. This approach increases frequency, but different media can also increase reach by appealing to different segments of the market or to different influencers or decision makers. Making decisions on reach versus frequency and continuous versus pulsing advertising strategies is part of this analysis. Figure 13.3 provides a checklist of considerations for making the decisions.

Develop Media Calendar   Finally, after examining costs and benefits of the various media types and combinations, put the entire media plan into calendar format for the year. (See Figure 7.4.) This accomplishes two things. First, it forces the product manager to think in advance. Second, by seeing the combinations of media in one place, the potential impact they have on each other can be improved. Third, the calendar helps focus on integrated marketing communications by incorporating nontraditional communications vehicles (e.g., seminars, newsletters, and software programs) into the plan. (See feature "Red Star Adopts Integrated Marketing Communications Program" on page 231.)

Creative Strategy

The creative strategy should include the basic message and positioning that should be communicated to the target market. Although an advertising agency might be responsible for the creative design of the adver-

	Objectives			
	Reach	Frequency	Continuity	Pulsing
Message Needs				
For new or highly complex message, strive for		•		
For dogmatic message, surge at beginning, then	•		•	
For reason-why messages, use high frequency at first, then				•
For emotionally oriented messages			•	
When message is so creative or product so newsworthy it forces attention	•			
When message is dull or product indistinguishable, strive for		•		
Customer purchase patterns				
To influence brand choice of regularly purchased products, use		•	•	
As purchase cycle lengthens, use		•		•
To influence erratic purchase cycles, strive for		•		•
To influence customer attitudes toward impulse purchases, use		•	•	
For products requiring great deliberation, alternate	•	•		
To reinforce customer loyalty, concentrate on	•		•	
To influence seasonal purchases, anticipate peak periods with	•	•		
Budget levels				
With a low budget, use				•
With a higher budget, strive for			•	

Figure 13.3 Setting Media Objectives

	Objectives			
	Reach	Frequency	Continuity	Pulsing
Competitive activity				
With heavy competitive advertising, concentrate on		●		
When competitive budgets are larger, use				●
Marketing objectives				
For new product introductions to mass market	●			
To expand share of market with new uses for product, use	●			
To stimulate direct response from advertising, use		●		●
To create awareness and recognition of corporate status, use	●		●	

Source: Courtland L. Bovee and William F. Arens, *Contemporary Advertising* (Burr Ridge, Ill.: Richard D. Irwin, 1982), 469

Figure 13.3 Setting Media Objectives (continued)

tising, the product manager should at least be able to critique it. As mentioned earlier, the advertising message depends on the positioning statement developed at the start of the planning process. The message should always be consistent with the positioning or unique selling proposition (USP) and include customer benefits that differentiate the product from the competition. Sometimes a company is interested in being positioned as innovative and uses patents to "prove" that position. Titleist has used its patented dimpling process to "prove" the quality of its golf balls; Samsonite luggage uses line drawings depicting patents and patents pending for the various product features.[2] In any case, the objective of the advertising is to convince potential customers that your

Red Star Adopts Integrated Marketing Communications Program

In the early 1990s, Red Star Specialty Products discovered that the messages reaching its trade customers were inconsistent. Their market of food technologists didn't know how Red Star products were different from competitors' products. Worse yet, only 10 percent of those responding to trade ads were "A" leads and 70 percent were "C" leads.

Since Red Star's $300,000 marketing budget could not be increased, it had to reevaluate where and how it spent its promotional dollars. First it scaled back its trade ads and used some of the money for educational materials, such as brochures, newsletters, and seminars. Another educational tool Red Star developed was an interactive software program with a tutorial on flavor enhancers and a guide to using specific products. These helped position Red Star as an advisor to food companies that had slashed their own R & D staff.

The company also developed an improved database to more effectively reach customers and prospects. According to Marketing Manager Tim Roebken, "Before, the most we had done is work with an industry magazine and do a direct mail piece to their list of subscribers. It was still a wasteful, mass-advertising approach. Of the 30,000 subscribers there may have been 5,000 or 6,000 we wanted to reach."

By examining problems and opportunities and acting on a specific positioning strategy, Red Star was able to increase the effectiveness of its marketing communications without increasing its total budget. The difference is that now two-thirds of the marketing budget is devoted to new vehicles (with only $100,000 spent on advertising), and all are integrated to provide a consistent message to the market.

Source: Adapted from Joe Mullich, "Red Star Crafts a New Marketing Recipe," *Business Marketing* (December 1994): 6+.

product is different from the competition in an important way and that this difference is strong enough to motivate them to buy.

For print advertising, the headline should attract prospects to the ad. Sometimes this can be done by stating the benefit or the promise of a reward. At other times, a provocative question will be more successful. The headline should generally maintain a positive tone and be coordinated with the rest of the ad. The copy should contain a benefit in the lead paragraph and use present-tense, active-voice words. If the copy is long, use subheads to make it easier on the eye. Identify what the prospect is to do as a result of reading the ad. Most business advertising (and a growing amount of consumer advertising) strives for direct response, so the copy should include the 800 number, the website URL, or other contact information. The layout should take eye movement into account and have a single dominant element rather than being overly cluttered.

For broadcast advertising, hold the number of elements to a minimum. Words should be conversational and concise. Take advantage of impact if using television commercials. With radio, be sure the company/product name is mentioned often.

For direct mail, set up repeated tests. Test different copy, different package formats, and different mailing lists. If possible, have a control to test against an alternative for each mailing. Personalize the cover letter and talk about the prospect's needs—not about the product. Use a strong offer to encourage people to respond. Do not simply encourage them to contact the company for more information; provide an incentive such as a free booklet, reduced price, or trial offer. If using direct mail (or any direct-response advertising), be sure to have inquiry fulfillment materials available. Highlight on the envelope that this is the information the prospect requested.

Include the salespeople in evaluating direct-response lead generation programs. Let them see the mail piece before it is mailed to customers and prospects, and ask them for input. Not only will salespeople offer useful suggestions, but they will also be more likely to buy into a program if brought in at the early stages.

Evaluating Advertising Effectiveness

Regardless of the medium used, collect as much data as possible on the return generated by each advertisement (return on promotional investment, ROPI). This will help determine which media are most effective and help in future budgeting. If advertising is done for long-term image reasons, periodically conduct image surveys to determine whether the investment is being well spent.

Sales Promotion

In addition to advertising, product managers might be involved with a variety of other promotional techniques, such as sampling, sales contests, and various other incentive programs. These are referred to as "incentive programs" because they provide inducements to stimulate short-term incremental sales of the product as opposed to building long-run brand loyalty. Promotions are commonly used to introduce new products, influence the effectiveness of competitors' tactics, or tap into a new market.

Product sampling can be an effective technique for encouraging customers to try a new product. New products that require behavioral change by potential users generally benefit from the ability of customers to try them on a low-cost or no-cost basis. 3M's Post-It Notes, for example, required free sampling for customers to experience using the product. Test drives are a method of sampling in the automotive industry. Rent-with-the-option-to-buy is a form of sampling that reduces cost (and risk) to both parties.

Distribution Strategy

Unless a product manager's products are distributed differently from all other products in the company, chances are he or she will not have significant control over strategic methods of distribution. Most of the activities will be related to working with the existing distributors, dealers, or agents and perhaps expediting shipments as necessary. However, some new products will necessitate changes in the channel of distribution, or market and competitive forces will require changes for existing products. This could also be a critical element of the plan if a product manager is rolling out a product into new regions and/or expanding globally. As a result, distribution strategy should not be ignored as the product manager develops the annual marketing plan.

Whenever a product manager introduces a lower-priced or higher-priced product, or one that has a different image, it might be necessary to introduce new channels. A potentially successful product can be thwarted by the wrong channel decision, as Huffy found when it introduced its new Cross Sport bike.

> Huffy Corp., for example, the successful $700 million bike maker, did careful research before it launched a new bicycle it dubbed the Cross Sport, a combination of the sturdy mountain bike popular with teenagers and the thin-framed, nimbler racing bike. Huffy conducted two separate series of market focus groups in shopping malls across the country, where randomly selected children and adults viewed the bikes and ranked them. The bikes met with shoppers' approval. So far, so good. In the summer of 1991, Cross Sports were shipped out to mass retailers, such as the Kmart and Toys 'R' Us chains, where Huffy already did most of its business. That was the mistake. As Richard L. Molen, Huffy president and chief executive, explains, the researchers missed one key piece of information. These special hybrid bikes were aimed at adults and, at $159, were priced 15 percent higher than other Huffy bikes, and therefore needed individual sales attention by the sort of knowledgeable salespeople who work only in bike specialty shops. Instead, Huffy's Cross Sports were supposed to be sold by the harried general salespeople at mass retailers such as Kmart. Result: "It was a $5 million mistake," says Molen. By 1992, the company had slashed Cross Sport production 7 percent and recorded an earnings drop of 30 percent.[3]

As markets fragment, different target customers—even for the same product—might seek alternative channels of distribution. Key accounts, for example, might best be served by going direct, whereas other customers can be more efficiently served through distributors. On the other hand, small customers might be handled by telesales, even if there are outside reps calling on larger customers in the same territory. Specialized distributors or agents might be more successful with certain segments than existing intermediaries, and that possibility should be periodically explored. Product managers will also need to evaluate the role of the Internet in Channel strategy.

Effectively motivating intermediaries can have a positive impact on the bottom line for the products. This starts by keeping a careful record of distributor or rep activity by product and assessing overall capabilities. Product managers should accompany regional or sales managers in routine visits to distributors or reps and might be expected to help prepare joint marketing plans. If there is an advisory council, the product manager should review the meeting minutes (at minimum the sections related to his or her product line) and react accordingly.

Manufacturers' and resellers' goals do not always match. Product managers sometimes tend to view resellers as the destination of their product. Resellers, on the other hand, view the receipt of a product as the beginning of a sales cycle. This can create unnecessary conflict, which can be reduced by a better sharing of information.

Product managers spend a good deal of money and effort to understand end-user needs and how their products fit these needs. Resellers should also be given this information. Providing this education to resellers not only helps them work better, but also enables them to provide valuable feedback to the manufacturer on product performance.

Product Support

Product support can encompass several things: installation, warranty follow-through, product upgrades, repairs, customer training, and so on. The product manager might not be directly involved with these activities, but he or she should be concerned about whether the policies and procedures are in place for them to happen. Customer satisfaction frequently depends as much on these factors as it does on the product itself. In addition, the product manager might be involved in developing services that optimize profit potential from various segments. We will examine some of the product support issues that a product manager might want to handle operationally or include in the marketing plan.

The cost of installation can be included in the price of the product or be an "optional" or unbundled component. The decision should be made in conjunction with the appropriate personnel (e.g., the service manager). If any significant changes are to be made, they should be mentioned in the marketing plan, with the impact on other marketing activities and on the bottom line.

A warranty or service contract can affect the salability of a product and should be examined along with other features. There are several questions to consider here:

- What do customers expect?
- Will there be a full or limited warranty?
- Can competitors match the warranty? Will they?

- Should the warranty be handled by the manufacturer, by the dealer, or by an independent organization?
- What are the advantages and disadvantages of service contracts and extended warranties?

As with any other part of the action program, changes to be implemented to the support program during the next fiscal year should be included in the marketing plan along with the impact and rationale.

Marketing Research

After completing the action program portion of the marketing plan, there will likely be information gaps that will require more data before the next planning cycle. This could include formal survey or focus group research, on-line database searching, and/or analysis of internal customer records and databases. If so, it is a good idea to include these activities as action items in the marketing plan to assure that resources and approvals have been attained. When a major project is expected, solicit proposals prior to the development of the action plan so that the time or cost of the project is not underestimated.

Checklist: Marketing Your Product

✓ Don't limit your marketing budget to advertising the same way you always have. Test new approaches and techniques.

✓ Be sure your communications reach the right people. It's better to have an average ad with a direct hit than a terrific ad shown to the wrong people.

✓ Experiment with database marketing to pinpoint the right message for the right customers.

✓ When creating print ads, strive to have a benefit or a reward in the headline.

✓ Integrate your marketing communications techniques to increase their effectiveness.

✓ Consider sales promotions as part of your marketing communications toolbox.

✓ Don't automatically assume that your current method of distribution is best for your product or that it won't require a change in the near future.

✓ Match the capabilities of your distributors or retailers with the selling requirements of your product.

✓ Monitor and control product support as a potential value-added component of your product.

14

Product Management: The Final Frontier?

PRODUCT MANAGEMENT HAS been evaluated, criticized, and applauded since its first introduction. Several writers have questioned whether product management will be a premier organizational structure in the future or whether it has become obsolete. Brand management, the most common form of product management in consumer goods companies, has perhaps come under the heaviest attack for several reasons. The availability of market data is unprecedented, causing brand managers to become overwhelmed. At the same time, senior managers demand more data to justify marketing decisions in the face of growing competition and a saturated market demand. Brand managers are being put under more scrutiny, with more and more decisions requiring higher management approval before progress can be made. Disillusionment with the system is high.

In other industries where product management has had a shorter history, the role is being viewed as a functional solution to several organizational problems. In particular, the approach is being implemented to provide the necessary match between the market's needs and the firm's ability to translate its core capabilities into products that satisfy these needs.

Regardless of the industry, product management is, and will continue to be, a viable organizational form. However, there will be modifications. Three variations to the original product management structure will likely play a role in the future for several companies. These variations—product management teams, more specialized focus, and a business unit manager approach—are discussed in this chapter.

Product Management Teams

The use of product management teams (PMTs) to make product-related decisions has grown recently. The specific role of the team, as well as its effectiveness, it still unclear. To put PMTs into perspective, it is useful to look at the evolution of teams in corporate America over the past decade or two and to provide some general categorization of teams.

The widespread use of teams started in the 1980s with the growth of quality circles used primarily in the auto and steel industries to combat Japanese competition. In general, workers and supervisors met intermittently to discuss quality problems and provide suggestions for *incremental* improvements. However, they rarely provided breakthrough thinking and began to lose their appeal. Nevertheless, the interest in teams continued, with the groups evolving into either worker teams or project teams:

> The teams most popular today are of two broad types: work teams, which include high-performance or self-managed teams, and special-purpose, problem-solving teams. Problem-solving teams, in particular, differ from quality circles in important ways. Where quality circles are permanent committees designed to handle whatever workplace problems may pop up, problem-solving teams have specific missions, which can be broad (find out why our customers hate us) or narrow (figure out why the No. 3 pump keeps overheating). Once the job is done, such teams usually disband.
>
> While problem-solving teams are temporary, work teams, used by about two-thirds of U.S. companies, tend to be permanent. Rather than attack specific problems, a work team does day-to-day work. A team of Boeing engineers helping to build a jet would be [an example of] a work team.[1]

The differences between the structure of the two types of teams are also worth noting. The project teams are frequently cross-functional, comprised of individuals representing the various operative areas related to the specific mission of the team. The work teams, although occasionally multifunctional, are more likely to have members who are similar in job function, with the authority to make decisions about how daily work is done.

The trouble with some PMTs being created today is that they combine the two structures, in effect developing an ongoing cross-functional team without a specific mission, yet without the ability to make decisions on daily workloads. This isn't meant to imply that teams cannot exist within a product management structure. Rather, a product manager should be prepared to work with *numerous* problem-solving teams on an ongoing basis rather than with one ongoing team.

Teams are critical in product-deletion decisions, issues related to establishing a consistent corporate image among all products in the company, work flow and scheduling, and new-product development. Each of these teams is likely to have different members and involve different time periods. The product manager takes on the role of integrator across these teams as they relate to the product line in question and is responsible for managing a bundle of projects at different stages of completion.

The company also plays a role in assuring that the various teams work together. If teams have to build consensus among both functional and team bosses, as at DEC, great time can be lost. On the other hand, empowering problem-solving teams to make immediate decisions can be both motivating and time-saving.

> [DEC announced in July 1994 that] it was abandoning its matrix team structure. Under the old system, workers in functional areas—engineering, marketing—also served on teams organized around product lines like minicomputers or integrated chips. The teams spent endless hours in meetings trying to build a consensus between the two factions in the matrix: the functional bosses and the team bosses. Its sheer organizational weight left DEC a laggard in the fast-moving technology sector.
>
> Boeing has an organizational structure similar to DEC's but with a critical difference. Its structure encourages teams to work together and seize initiative. Says Henry Shomber, a Boeing chief engineer: "We have the no-messenger rule. Team members must make decisions on the spot. They can't run back to their functions for permission." This kind of freedom allowed Boeing to use teams to build its new 777 passenger jet, which flew its first successful test flight this summer [1994] with fewer than half the number of design glitches of earlier programs.[2]

More Specialized Focus

Given the growing responsibilities assigned to product managers, some companies are questioning whether there is simply too much for one individual to handle. As a result, there has been movement toward narrowing the focus of the product manager. The type of focus is company- or industry-specific. A number of fast-moving consumer-goods (FMCG) companies, for example, have split the product manager position into two areas of specialization. One manager focuses on consumer issues, and the other focuses on trade issues. Del Monte followed this type of reorganization in 1993. "The intent is to become more of a specialist," said Christine Di Fillippo, brand manager of tomato products at Del Monte.[3]

The ability to deal with the trade is likely to continue to escalate in importance. Although retail giants have existed for a long time, their clout has increased due to the emergence of powerful information systems that provide them with more data on consumers than manufacturers have. Consumer-goods manufacturers are finding it necessary to organize around their customers (the retailers), invest in technology, and act more as a partner than was typical in the past. Vendors to Wal-Mart have to respond to a barrage of demands to get their product sold (or even on the shelves). Companies are also increasingly including retailer input at the early stages of product development. Black & Decker solicited input from several retailers, including Home Depot, when it introduced the DeWalt line of power tools. The president of Black & Decker's power tools group emphasized their involvement: "We talked to them about the name. We talked to them about the color. We talked to them about the warranty."[4] Their input was valuable not only in terms of product design, but also as a visible sign of their involvement as a partner.

Other FMCG companies have restructured to allow the brand manager to focus more specifically on product issues, with advertising handled under a corporate umbrella. There is some logic to this approach when a company brand identity is more important to the market than the brand image of the line or item over which the product manager has control. However, unless the product has unique technical demands, the position of product manager might not be necessary in this situation, and a functional organization could suffice.

Some highly technical companies have taken a similar route, having product managers focus on the engineering and technical aspects of a product, with most marketing decisions handled by a separate function. In this case, the product manager may become a technical/applications expert with the job of helping the salespeople, while the other individual is responsible for understanding the market and communicating product benefits to them. The risk of separating marketing from development is that the product manager loses contact with the customer and becomes too close to the product to be objective.

Whatever attempts are made at specialization to make the product manager's job more manageable, it's critical to remember why the position was created in the first place: to better understand the product and its competition so that customer needs are satisfied.

Business Unit Manager

Other companies have reorganized into what are essentially business units, with the product manager responsible for the general management of the product line. This is a type of team arrangement that elaborates on the product management team (PMT) concept but in a sense allows a more specialized focus on the product as a business. Under this type of structure, the product manager assumes more responsibility for all of the business functions related to the product, going well beyond the marketing and planning.

> While the product manager has always worked in a spectrum ranging from marketing specialist to general manager, the business unit structure places greater emphasis on the general management side.
>
> Jennifer Kan at Specialty Brands is part of this new kind of team and has new responsibilities over areas such as finance and inventory. "Companies seem to be searching for the next generation of organizations, trying to figure out what will work best in the upcoming years," she said.[5]

If product managers are to be held fully accountable for the success of their products, it's reasonable to expect them to be given sufficient authority to facilitate success. The business unit manager structure makes that possible. However, it also requires that the person hired for the position has the experience, reputation, and respect to carry it out.

Other Trends

There are at least two trends likely to impact the future of product management, particularly in larger firms. One is the growth of global megabrands. The other is the dramatic metamorphosis of distribution channels and logistics management.

The globalization of brands is occurring in both consumer and business arenas. Kelly Services, a temporary worker agency, has both domestic and international locations. Coca-Cola, Sony, and Levi Strauss are brand names recognized throughout the world. Companies are realizing they have to accept this movement toward global brands as inevitable.

> Major brand companies frequently inform the media that globalization is their most pressing challenge. The year 1990 saw a series of acquisitions and (more commonly) mergers because companies felt the need to expand in order to compete in a global market: Hoffman La Roche and Genetic or Merck and Du Pont in pharmaceuticals; AT&T and NCR in computers; Matsushita and MCA in entertainment electronics; Whirlpool and Philips in white goods; Asahi and Elders IXL in beer. Procter & Gamble's chairman Edwin L. Arztz offered these words at the company's general meeting in 1990: "The acquisition strategy will be driven by globalization, which will be the principle engine of growth in sales. It's not optional. That's the way business will be done."[6]

What does this mean for product managers? Many product managers will be challenged to understand market needs for their products beyond American borders. The transition for some companies will be minor if few changes are required to the product or its marketing. In other cases, extensive marketing research, product adaptation, and promotional modifications will be unavoidable. The product manager may also be required to work with company personnel located at plants or offices in other countries, sometimes coordinating virtual teams through videoconferencing, fax, and other electronic means. These cross-border business teams will be responsible for leveraging corporate capabilities throughout the world.

The proliferation of different channels for both consumer and business products, from club stores to distribution alliances to direct marketing, might pressure manufacturers to offer broad and varied product lines. In addition to these diverse ways of reaching customers, logistics management also includes the relationships with suppliers to get the right parts and products to your company as effectively and efficiently as possible. These factors can have a profound and strategic impact on the success of a product manager's offering.

> Just how strategic? Compaq Computer, the white-hot company that recently became the world's number one producer of PCs, estimates it lost $500 million to $1 billion in sales [in 1994] because its laptops and desktops weren't available when and where customers were ready to buy them. Says chief financial officer Daryl White: "We've done most of what we need to do to be more competitive. We've changed the way we develop products, manufacture, market, and advertise. The one piece of the puzzle we haven't addressed is logistics. It's the next source of competitive advantage. The possibilities are just astounding."[7]

Product managers must realize the impact of the distribution channel (both in and out of the company) in affecting the success of the product line. The implication for the product manager is the need to solicit input from a wider spectrum of "customers," including suppliers, purchasing staff, and logistics and transportation personnel.

Concluding Remarks

Product management is here to stay. The position is challenging, demanding, and rewarding. Product managers will be given more responsibilities as the challenges of going to market increase. Some companies will experiment with product management teams or a narrowing of job focus for product managers or a business unit approach, but the companies for whom the structure is most successful will hire, groom, and empower product managers to create products with both internal integrity from a design perspective and external integrity from a customer perspective.

Regardless of the organizational changes product management goes through in the future, successful product managers will have a thorough understanding of the various segments within a market (including global segments), an understanding of the "core competencies" available to the company, and the ability to leverage these competencies to meet market needs. In other words, the product manager of the future will have the ability to attain customer satisfaction by serving as a cross-functional leader in the firm.

Case Four[1]

The 3M ScotchCart®II Cartridge

THE 3M SCOTCHCART®II cartridge was a broadcast cartridge tape for prerecorded radio messages introduced in 1986 by 3M's broadcasting and related products department. Product manager Bill Parfitt developed a marketing plan for it that highlighted the tactics most appropriate for increasing the cartridge's sales volume. According to Parfitt, "You must have a marketing plan to follow to be effective. With a plan, you are 90 percent proactive and 10 percent reactive. Without a plan, you are 90 percent reactive and 10 percent proactive. Even if a plan is not required, do one. It will save a tremendous amount of work."

The marketing tactics called for sales support products/activities, flexible pricing policies, trade shows, and print advertising.

Sales Support

3M's toolbox of support items for the sales force was extensive. Some of these were provided routinely, while others were developed and made available on an as-needed basis. The product reference guide was an important piece of information for the sales force. It contained a brief product description, an opening sales statement, and opening and follow-up questions to help salespeople qualify needs. The next page of the reference guide contained common problems broadcasters might experience with tapes—and the resulting consequences—to enable the reps to customize the 3M product to the customer's needs. Although not all items are used with each product, many of these were provided for the ScotchCart®II cartridge.

As part of the marketing tactics, Parfitt made sure the sales force was informed of marketing activities before they were seen by the customer, and they always received a sample of giveaways in advance.

3M supplied the following materials to its sales force:

- Comprehensive product/application/ market manuals
- History timelines
- Information on special accounts
- Complete pricing, including special pricing

- Brochures
- Advertisement reprints
- Article reprints
- Technical bulletins
- Competitive comparisons
- Promotion outlines
- Product reference guide
- Newsletters
- Complete set of policy pages
- Complete dealer information
- List of key accounts or new prospects
- Buying-pattern information
- Market-research data
- Competitive brochures, ads, PR, etc.
- Glossary of industry terms
- Video training tapes
- Yearbooks
- Directories
- Flow charts
- Market-application charts

Flexible Pricing Policies

Radio stations, the target market for these 3M products, including the ScotchCart®II, were under pressure to conserve working capital while also needing to acquire sophisticated, technologically advanced equipment. 3M responded with several extended payment plans. The standard lease offered thirty-six-, forty-eight-, or sixty-month pay-for-use plans on total purchases exceeding $5,000. The options available at the end of the lease included purchasing the equipment for the estimated market value, renewing the lease, or returning the equipment. The prime rate lease purchase plan provided financing for a twelve- to thirty-six-month term, with the title to the equipment transferring automatically upon completion of the final payment; the interest rate for the program was based on the current prime lending rate published each day in *The Wall Street Journal*.

In addition to the lease program, 3M used price actively in gaining customers both directly and through distribution. Special prices were developed for customer-special versions, partially based on the added value to the customers. Monetary incentives were also used to encourage dealers to switch their broadcasting customers from a competitive product to a 3M product. A 5 percent switcher/finder's fee was allocated for this purpose.

Trade Shows

Trade shows were also used as a tactic for gaining awareness and preference for the product. Parfitt started by compiling a list of shows relevant to the potential market for the ScotchCart®II and then obtaining performance data on the shows.

Several decisions had to be made regarding the potential attendance at the trade shows. Should inquiry cards or brochures be provided? How many? Should giveaways, incentives, or contests be part of the plan? What types? Should a preshow mailer be sent to potential attendees? Who would be responsible for each activity?

Recognizing that trade shows are more than three-dimensional ads, Parfitt put together a trade show plan. For an example of the type of planning tool that can be used, see Figure 14.1. This information not only highlights the activities that need to be controlled for an effective trade show, but it also lists the individuals responsible for making them happen.

Print Advertising

The advertising for the ScotchCart®II cartridge was designed to emphasize that the product lasted longer than the competition while delivering consistently high performance. In the ads, the product was centrally positioned with significant features pointed out through the use of arrows. *Business Marketing* evaluated the first ad of this series in its Copy Chasers column:

> 3M, always a strong contender in any advertising judging, caught our eye with an excellent invitation to "Discover the secrets to a longer life" for its broadcast cartridges (tape cartridges carrying prerecorded radio station messages, commercials and the like). The product cutaway and call-outs tell the entire product feature story, backing up the promise in the headline.[2]

Two other ads in the campaign continued the use of consistent layout and message. All carried the headline on top, the product cutaway in the center with call-out features on each side, two columns of copy at the bottom, with the 3M logo in the bottom right corner.

In order to get approval on the marketing communications expenditure required, Parfitt used supporting effectiveness ratios from an Advertising Research Foundation study. A formula built on this information was presented in *Business Marketing* for estimating return on promotional investment. The ROPI formula is

$$\text{Leads} \times \text{Inserts} \times (45\%) \times \text{Market share} \%$$
$$\times \text{Average sales amount} = \text{Sales}$$

The 45 percent figure in the formula is based on the results of two studies. The Inquiry Handling Service Inc., in analyzing 10,000 leads from fifteen different business-to-business companies found that 21 percent bought some company's product within six months and 31 percent were still budgeted to buy within the year. A prior Advertising Research Foundation report (Report No. 25) cited similar ratios of buyers. The number of leads per insert is based on the uniqueness of the product, the effectiveness of the insert, and similar variables; your best estimate of the figure can be obtained from your own company's past experience. The market share and average sales amount can be obtained from internal documents.

According to James Obermayer,

> The rules for the ROPI are simple: 22% or slightly more of inquirers will buy within six months; around 45% of them will buy someone's product within one year. Furthermore, your company's share of those sales will usually be your market share in the industry.
>
> For example, suppose each insertion (magazine insertions or direct mail waves) produces 30 leads and the media plan calls for 12 insertions. We expect 45% of those leads to buy within a year. Knowing or estimating market share at 36%, and knowing the average sale produces $950 revenue, we forecast total sales of $55,404 from the leads generated by the ads. From that point, it's very easy to predict cost per raw lead and a cost per closed lead.[3]

Several techniques were built into the program to help track the campaign. Bingo cards (reply cards inserted into a publication for readers to request literature from companies whose products and services are advertised) were used where appropriate. In other cases, steps were taken to ensure inquiries were routed to the product manager.

Description	Responsible	Projected Completion Date	Date Completed
Set objectives			
Gather show information			
Show selection			
Contract for space			
Exhibit design			
Exhibit construction			
Freight			
Drayage			
Set-up			
Electrical			
Plumbing			
Telephone			
Furniture rental			
Janitorial service			
Photography			
Guard service			
Florist service			
A/V equipment			
Presenters/models			
Inquiry cards			
Literature			
Equipment			
Badges			
Rooms			
Directory copy			
Suite			
Invitations			
Preshow promotion			
Booth staffing			

Figure 14.1 Trade Show Responsibilities

Description	Responsible	Projected Completion Date	Date Completed
Prizes			
Giveaways			
Budget projection			
Show evaluation form			
Inquiry follow-up			
Postshow follow-up			
Audit and pay-related invoices			
Miscellaneous			

Figure 14.1 Trade Show Responsibilities (continued)

Conclusion

The marketing tactics for the ScotchCart®II as well as other 3M products were based on an integrated approach to planning. Objectives were established to guide the implementation of the plan. All possible promotional vehicles were considered as viable elements of the marketing communications. Pricing was built into the plan rather than simply being an after-the-plan reaction. And finally, sales promotion, in the form of free sampling, was incorporated to help the market gain rapid experience with the product.

As for other product managers, the message is clear. The first step is to identify the problems and opportunities for a given product that should trigger planning items for the next fiscal year. These problems and opportunities must then be converted into objectives for the marketing plan. Based on the objectives, a target market must be selected for the product and a positioning strategy developed to differentiate the product from the competition in the minds of that target market. Finally, specific tactics (pricing, marketing communications, logistics, product support) need to be acted on to solidify the positioning in the customers' minds and accomplish the fiscal-year objectives.

APPENDIX:
SAMPLE JOB DESCRIPTIONS

THIS APPENDIX CONTAINS actual job descriptions from companies in a variety of industries.

Job Description in a Biotechnology Firm

Title: Senior Product Manager, DNA Purification

Reports to: Director, Product/Marketing Management

Duties:

1. Develop long-term marketing plan for business/customer focus area (includes many product lines), determining what products to add to the line and the short-term and long-term marketing mix that will result in maximum growth of the product line (i.e., promotions needed, publicity, training and support, pricing, image of product).

2. Prepare and give group presentations on marketing and sales strategy and proposed new product development, including ROI (return on investment) calculations, competitive analysis, customer needs, critical success factors, market analysis, sales justification, and other components outlined in the standard business plan template.

3. Initiate and negotiate contracts and licenses for new technologies, products, or kits using standard process and coordinating, as appropriate, with research and development, legal, corporate development, and manufacturing departments after corporate approval.

4. Initiate and follow up on original equipment manufacturer (OEM) opportunities by meeting with OEM suppliers and meeting with the legal department to discuss and approve terms and give sales estimates. Identify potential products and customers to purchase company products on OEM basis. Discuss and approve pricing with OEM sales staff.

5. Prepare annual marketing budget for the business area. Responsible for keeping spending within budgetary limits.

6. Evaluate the marketing side of possible new technologies presented by corporate development and other groups, completing the evaluation checklist in the company intranet. Identify potential technologies needed for the strategic direction of product line for corporate development to pursue. Negotiate licensing terms, as needed.

7. Provide leadership, training, coaching, and/or mentoring to one or more product managers, including giving input into hiring, development, and evaluation processes for these staff.

8. Give final approval on pricing guidelines for distributors and direct customers, within pricing strategy and pricing policies. Ensure that pricing has been approved by the appropriate internal group.

9. Attend trade shows as marketing representative, as needed. Responsible for setting trade show theme and managing booth on-site. Work with trade show coordinator on booth happenings and logistics.

10. Approve final language used in catalog. Train others in features and benefits to be used for catalog text, as needed. Work with external staff on overall product image plan for catalog.

11. Ensure that all goals and objectives of the marketing and sales plan for the business area are met by continually monitoring and reporting on product trends, competitive trends, sales trends, financial changes, and other problem areas. Recommend and lead alternative actions as needed to meet overall objectives of short-term and long-term plan.

12. Understand and comply with all elements of the company quality system outlined for the position.

Qualifications:

1. B.S. in appropriate scientific area or B.S. in marketing with concentrated training in appropriate scientific area; seven years in marketing position, including at least three years in product or marketing management or sales.

2. Proven ability to effectively communicate with several types and levels of staff and external contacts, both in writing and verbally. Effective presentation skills.

3. Ability to effectively work simultaneously on many priorities, which change frequently.

4. Thorough knowledge of all financial components of product and marketing management, including product contribution margins, profit and loss statements, budget processes, and return on investment calculations.

5. Thorough knowledge of contracting and licensing process. Ability to effectively negotiate terms and conditions for licenses and contracts with outside parties.

Job Description in a Biotechnology Firm

Title: Product Manager, Cell Regulation

Reports to: Manager, Product Management

Duties:

1. Responsible for product logistics of assigned product line, including entering information into company system (and accuracy of information entered by others), printing labels, finalizing pricing, completing packaging, and preparing literature and distributor/branch notifications for all new products. Pricing involves analysis of pricing of similar company and competitor products and recommended process to marketing managers and group leader for review and approval. Packaging involves determining appropriate packaging after review and input from research and development staff and recommendation and approval by marketing managers.

2. Notify branch office staff, distributors, and internal staff of new product introductions by sending internal notification, standard forms, and sales summary (as reviewed by senior product manager or marketing manager).

3. Implement trademark searches for approved trade names.

4. Develop monthly progress reports on all products within area of responsibility, including sales for product line, trends, monthly advertising and promotion schedule, and competitive information by the third day of each month. Follow monthly report format.

5. Input information into computer system and run sales analysis on product line, as requested. Demonstrate proficiency with senior product manager review.

6. Coordinate responses to daily faxes and E-mails. Mail and send daily replies.

7. Assist group with annual marketing plan, strategic plan, and budget.

8. Provide quotes to customers as needed (after review by product marketing manager).

9. Proofread catalog section for accuracy in text, pricing, trademarks, and so on.

10. Prepare monthly analyses of spending activities and provide them for the marketing managers.

11. Assist more experienced product managers with focus groups. Specifically, recruit participants, arrange logistics, and pay attendees (if needed).

12. Assist others in identifying outside sources for contract and OEM licensing. May prepare draft marketing issues for inclusion in contract/licensing.

13. Assist with special projects (i.e., conducting customer surveys by telephone or Internet).

14. Attend weekly product manager meeting.

15. Understand and comply with all elements of the company quality system outlined for the position.

Qualifications:

1. B.S. in appropriate scientific area, or in marketing with concentrated training in appropriate scientific area. One year in marketing related position or utilizing marketing skills.

2. Strong written and verbal communication skills, including technical writing.

3. Ability to work simultaneously on many priorities, which change frequently.

Job Description in a Consumer Product Firm

Title: Assistant Product Manager, Clothing

Reports to: Product Manager, Clothing

Purpose: Responsible for the promotional clothing business for the company family of brands. Responsibility covers executing all merchandising and design functions, communicating product availability, and timely task completion.

Duties:

1. Work with product manager of clothing, marketing and sales departments, outside design resources, and vendors in all aspects of line development, including line planning, color, product selection, fit styling, product sourcing, and manufacturability.

2. Develop detailed line plan for each brand.

3. Secure sourcing for each product to maximize customer value and profit objectives.

4. Analyze product costing and establish product pricing for promotional products to balance corporate gross margin goals with market demand and positioning.

5. Develop initial product forecasts to determine profitability of each line and examine impact of adding additional products to the line.

6. Initiate timetable for development of promotional product lines to ensure introduction during the appropriate time frame to maximize sales and minimize carrying costs.

7. Present promotional clothing line to management, sales force, and other internal departments.

8. Interface with subsequent departments to minimize production/ development problems and determine product needs.

9. Coordinate the distribution of samples to sales force and ensure the development of all coordinating sales tools, including but not limited to catalogs and dealer flyers.

10. Prepare booking analysis for promotional products on a quarterly basis to aid in planning the introduction of future products.

Secondary Duties:

1. Execute the development of special products for promotional and team needs.

2. Communicate with sales force to determine seasonal product, price, and forecast needs.

3. Maintain boards of promotional products for each line.

4. Distribute line information to applicable internal departments, including sales, marketing, international, and the company stores.

5. Interface with all appropriate vendors to communicate product development timetables and initial forecasts. Initiate new product development.

6. Maintain product plans and cost/detail sheets for each product.

7. Input travel/budget needs to product manager, clothing.

8. Additional duties as assigned by product manager, clothing.

Qualifications:

1. B.S. or B.A. degree in business administration/merchandising.

2. Minimum two years retail and/or product development experience.

3. Outstanding communication and presentation skills.

4. Well-developed organizational and human relations skills.

5. Ability to establish and maintain multiple priorities.

6. Ability to function in a team environment.

7. Working knowledge of forecasting techniques, percentages, and mark-ups.

8. Working knowledge of computer programs including Excel and Word.

Physical Requirement:

Domestic and international travel required.

Job Description in an Industrial Capital Equipment Firm

Title: Product Manager, Drying and Air Systems

Department: Paper Group

Reports to: Director, Product Management

Summary: Provide overall management of the designated products. Provide product direction and vision. Responsible for implementing product development process, reducing product cost, and ensuring worldwide product standards. Work with sales, marketing research, production engineering, product analysis, and central standards departments, as well as manufacturing site, field service, and applications groups.

Duties:

1. Has single-source responsibility for developing and implementing global product strategy and market positioning for the designated product, in each grade.

2. Coordinate selection of products for development. Organize and coordinate product development process for the designated product. Coordinate product development work and research activities.

3. Responsible for costs, features, performance, reliability, maintenance, and manufacturability. Work with capital manufacturing and purchasing to achieve cost objectives. Develop and document global design, safety, and performance standards.

4. Work with sales and service organizations to maximize product performance and achieve revenue objectives. Ensure that customers are satisfied with product performance. Use market feedback for product improvements and new product development process.

5. Supervise the market assessments, competitive evaluations, product development activities, identification of customer needs and perceptions, management of product database, and preparation of sales and marketing materials and product

training programs. Continuously monitor competitive offerings, maintain knowledge of competitive features, and incorporate competitive features, as appropriate.

6. Direct planning of each product development activity and assist in the preparation of the strategic plan for the designated product.

7. Establish and maintain an effective staff, evaluate employee performance, administer group wages, determine workforce requirements, maintain global communications, and promote group training and technical competence.

8. Help establish and manage group operating budget and keep product development costs on each product's activities within the plan limits.

Job Description in a Telecommunications Organization

Title: Product Manager/Team Leader

Department: Product Marketing

Division: Marketing

Status: Exempt

Reports to: Product Marketing Manager

Supervises: Associate Product Managers

Summary: Manage, promote, direct, plan, and coordinate activities for specific product line and ensure synergy with related product line managers on the team to ensure that product line objectives are accomplished within prescribed time frame and parameters.

Quality Statement: Promote total quality management. Demonstrate and encourage the importance of internal and external customer satisfaction and quality work.

Duties:

1. Responsible for managing, promoting, directing, and controlling related product line, which includes but is not limited to the following duties:
   - establishing product line direction for existing products, including product line extensions and additional target markets;
   - marketing/promoting product line;
   - supporting and training sales staff;
   - devising sales channel strategies;
   - tracking revenue and margin;
   - pricing markets and targeting strategies and discount structures;
   - initiating measures for product cost containment and cost reduction (due diligence with engineering and operations);
   - tracking industry trends, product segment growth, market share;

- ensuring synergy and cohesive approach to execution and communication by the team members to support the overall product family objective.

2. Establish clear pricing strategies, discount structures, and guidelines for all sales channels and target markets.

3. Prioritize engineering development and promotional projects for the product line.

4. Manage product line direction through an ongoing assessment of current products, pricing, and position; systematically develop and evaluate opportunities for new products and/or line extensions; and identify new target markets (jointly with industry marketing) and related strategies.

5. Document concept for new products and/or line extensions to meet existing or anticipated market needs and present to manager and/or research and development committee as appropriate, according to the established product development process. Develop market opportunity document; document product specifications required (PRD); initiate and prioritize the project within engineering; track product development through project engineering; plan, develop, and communicate strategy for product launch and initial forecast; track sales, costs, and margin and effects on existing product line revenues; and conduct continued product promotion.

6. Develop, execute, and maintain product and product family business plan that provides current market information, including sales and gross profit margin history, year-to-date (YTD) actuals and projections, key market positioning, sales channels and competitive strategies, pricing, market share, product life cycle plans, and evolution plans.

7. Initiate and participate in the development of all marketing collateral, including website and catalog pages, product releases, brochures, advertisements, video, PC presentations, special premium items, flyers. Establish sales promotions and special incentive programs.

8. Support sales force through joint sales calls to key accounts; proposal/bid volume pricing and development assistance; and trade show support and conference calls. Develop and conduct product, market, and application training. Communicate product line updates and key information in weekly update; E-mail to sales force and key employees.

9. Establish final pricing of the product, including list price, discount structure, and special price incentives, on a global scale.

10. Maintain an awareness of the competition and other market forces affecting the product line, through effective networking and mainstream research. Provide key competitive information and product comparisons to market research team for the timely maintenance and publication of the competitive product information manual, adding information as required and ensuring accuracy and accessibility to key employees.

11. Provide and/or present monthly, quarterly, and annual product line update reports as directed.

12. Provide supervision, training, ongoing guidance, and mentorship to assigned personnel in accomplishing their objectives and fulfilling their responsibilities. Monitor their progress and participate in performance review process for assigned personnel, as appropriate. Interview potential candidates and assist in hiring decisions.

13. Assist in leading the day-to-day activities of the department to achieve both the corporate and departmental objectives.

14. Encourage continuous process improvement by developing ways to maximize each team member's involvement in all process improvements.

15. Assist in special projects and/or perform additional duties that are assigned.

16. Demonstrate and encourage a cooperative and congenial working relationship, within and outside the company.

Qualifications:

1. Bachelor's degree in marketing, business, or a technical field, or an equivalent combination of education and technical/professional experience.

2. Three years of product marketing experience in telecommunications or a related technical industry.

3. Demonstrated ability to lead and organize cross-functional meetings, committees, and people in a professional manner.

4. Demonstrated aggressive, persuasive, and creative problem-solving skills.

5. Excellent verbal and written communication, presentation, organization, and time-management skills.

6. Proficient use of word processing, spreadsheet, presentation, and E-mail software.

Job Description in a Mid-Sized Industrial Firm

Title: Manager/General Aftermarket

Department: Marketing

Reports to: Director of Marketing

Purpose: Serve customers and develop products and markets by assessing customer needs, establishing and implementing tactical market plans, developing and/or finding sources for required products, and establishing longer-term strategic plans.

Duties:

1. Service existing accounts and establish new accounts by planning and organizing a daily work schedule that maintains contact with existing and potential customers and establishes new customers.

2. Facilitate the sale of current products through existing channels by establishing promotional programs, recommending advertising venues, participating in trade shows, calling on customers with field sales representatives, evaluating sales-call results, and providing a liaison role with other product and market managers.

3. Pursue new-product and market opportunities by comparing company products, services, and capabilities to those of competitors regarding markets, price, new products, delivery, advertising, and merchandising techniques. Gather current information on total and served market, market share, and growth opportunities.

4. Increase aftermarket sales by developing and/or finding sources of new products to position company for growth.

5. Determine product pricing by reviewing costs, anticipating volume, and utilizing competitive market research data.

6. Provide liaison in new products by coordinating product development and sourcing programs. Establish and follow up on completion date requirements.

7. Evaluate existing distribution channels in relationship to company capabilities and current and potential competitive position.

8. Resolve customer complaints by investigating problems, developing solutions, preparing reports, and making recommendations to management when necessary.

9. Suggest advertising and sales promotion programs by reviewing and evaluating current and previous company programs' effectiveness and programs offered by competitors.

10. Keep management informed by submitting activity and results reports, such as call reports and monthly significant developments. Prepare short- and long-term product sales forecasts and special reports and analyses. Answer questions and requests.

11. Maintain inter- and intra-departmental work flow by fostering the spirit of cooperation.

12. Contribute to team effort by accomplishing related results and completing special projects as assigned by management.

ENDNOTES

Preface

1. Book reviews, the *Journal of Product Innovation Management* (14: 4, July 1997), 314.

Chapter 1

1. Zachary Schiller, "The Marketing Revolution at Procter & Gamble," *Business Week* (July 25, 1988): 72.
2. Jean E. LeGrand, "A Product in Need of Management," *Bankers Magazine* 175 (November/December 1992): 73+.
3. William J. Wichman, "Product Management as a Marketing Strategy," *National Underwriter* (July 29, 1991): 10+.
4. G. M. Naidu, A. Kleimenhagen, and G. D. Pillari, "Is Product-Line Management Appropriate for Your Health Care Facility?" *Journal of Health Care Marketing* 13 (Fall 1993): 8.
5. Ibid., 10.
6. Eric Berggren and Robert Dewar, "Is Product Management Obsolete?" *Journal of Retail Banking* 13 (Winter 1991/1992): 27+.
7. Based on information from a proprietary survey conducted by the author.

Chapter 2

1. Regina Fazio Maruca, "The Right Way to Go Global," *Harvard Business Review* (March/April 1994): 137.

2. P. L. Dawes and P. G. Patterson, "The Performance of Industrial and Consumer Product Managers," *Industrial Marketing Management*, 17 (February 1988): 73–84.

3. Ibid., 83.

4. Bill Meserve, "The Changing Role of Product Management," *Electronic Business* (January 9, 1989): 146.

5. William Weilbacher, *Brand Marketing* (Lincolnwood, Ill.: NTC Business Books, 1993), 123.

Chapter 3

1. The information in this section is adapted from Kim B. Clark and Takahiro Fujimoto, "The Power of Product Integrity," *Harvard Business Review* (November–December 1990): 107–118; Christopher Power, "Flops," *Business Week* (16 August, 1993): 76–82; Kathleen Kerwin, "GM's Aurora," *Business Week* (21 March, 1994): 88–95; and Jean E. LeGrand, "A Product in Need of Management," *Banker Magazine* (November–December 1992): 73–76.

Case One

1. My thanks to Chuck West of *West & Associates* (Minneapolis) for his insights on sales training. (westx033@tc.umn.edu)

2. John Monoky, "Is Your Time Well Spent?" *Industrial Distribution* (February 1, 1997): 83.

3. Don Frey, "Learning the Ropes: My Life as a Product Champion," *Harvard Business Review* 69 (September/October 1991): 54.

4. Robert W. Koehler, "Triple-Threat Strategy," *Management Accounting* 72 (October 1991): 32.

5. Ralph S. Blois, "Do You Really Need an Agency?" *Sales & Marketing Management* 140 (October 1988): 120.

Chapter 4

1. Condensed from E-mail message from John Schramm, July 30, 1998.

2. Statement in E-mail message from Joe Pigeon, July 7, 1998.

3. Statement in E-mail message from Mark Mulvihill, July 1, 1998.

4. My thanks to Stephan Spencer (sspencer@netconcepts.com) and John McConnell (JohnMack@aol.com) for their contributions to this section.

5. Several companies currently market customer relationship management software. Examples include Onyx, Baan, and Vantive. Check their websites for further information.
6. Patricia B. Seybold, "Customers.com: How to Create a Profitable Business Strategy for Internet and Beyond," *Times Business*, (1998): 39.
7. Ed M. Yavuz and Daniel Heidelman, "Knowledge Management: The 'Office Water Cooler' of the 21st Century," *Medical Marketing and Media* 34 (April 1999): 66–70.
8. Again, thanks to Stephan Spencer for sharing this example.
9. John Gallaugher, "Challenging the New Conventional Wisdom of Net Commerce Strategies," *Association for Computing Machinery, Communications of the ACM* 42 (July 1999): 27–29.

Chapter 5

1. Gary Hamel and C. K. Prahalad, "Strategic Intent," *Harvard Business Review* 67 (May/June 1989): 63–76.
2. Marian B. Wood and Evelyn Ehrlich, "Segmentation: Five Steps to More Effective Business Marketing," *Sales & Marketing Management* 143 (April 1991): 59.

Chapter 6

1. Alan W. H. Grant and Leonard A. Schlesinger, "Realize Your Customers' Full Profit Potential," *Harvard Business Review* 73: 5 (September–October 1995): 61–62.

Chapter 7

1. Betsy D. Gelb, "Why Rich Brands Get Richer, and What to Do About It," *Business Horizons* 35 (September–October 1992): 46.

Case Two

1. The information from this section is adapted from Sharen Kindel, "Selling by the Book," *Sales & Marketing Management* (October 1994): 101–107; David Woodruff and Karen Lowry Miller, "Chrysler's Neon," *Business Week* (May 3, 1993): 116–126; Patrick Bedard, "Dodge Neon," *Car and Driver* (April 1994): 55–59; and Neon promotional literature..

Chapter 8

1. James R. Tindall, "Marketing Established Brands," *Journal of Consumer Marketing* 8 (Fall 1991): 5–10.
2. Jeremy Main, "How to Steal the Best Ideas Around," *Fortune* (October 19, 1992): 103.
3. Ibid.

Chapter 9

1. Regina Fazio Maruca, "The Right Way to Go Global," *Harvard Business Review* 72 (March/April 1994): 143.
2. "The Knowledge-Creating Company," *Harvard Business Review* 69 (November/December 1991): 101.
3. Brian Dumaine, "Closing the Innovation Gap," *Fortune* (December 2, 1991): 59.
4. Kathleen Kerwin, "GM's Aurora," *Business Week* (March 21, 1994): 88–95.

Chapter 10

1. Christopher Power, Kathleen Kerwin, Keith Alexander, and Robert D. Hof, "Flops," *Business Week* (August 16, 1993): 79.
2. Peter Strub and Steven Herman, "Can the Sales Force Speak for the Customer?" *Marketing Research* (Fall 1993) 5, no. 4, 32–35.
3. Kathleen Kerwin, "GM's Aurora," *Business Week* (March 21, 1994): 88–95.
4. Faye Rice, "Secrets of Product Testing," *Fortune* (November 28, 1994): 166–172.
5. C. Merle Crawford, *New Products Management*, 4th ed. (Burr Ridge, Ill.: Richard D. Irwin, 1994): 351.
6. Bruce Nussbaum and Robert Neff, "I Can't Work This Thing!" *Business Week* (April 29, 1991): 60.
7. C. Merle Crawford, *New Products Management*, 4th ed. (Homewood, Ill.: Richard D. Irwin, 1994): 351–353.

Case Three

1. The information in this section is adapted from Robert Hof, "Intel: Far Beyond the Pentium," *Business Week* (February 20, 1995): 88–90; Tim Clark, "Intel Sets $8 Million Campaign," *Business Marketing* (Febru-

ary 1994): 1, 40; John Quelch and David Kenny, "Extend Profits, Not Product Lines," *Harvard Business Review* (September–October 1994): 153–160; Stephen Kreider Yoder, "How H-P Used Tactics of the Japanese to Beat Them at Their Game," *Wall Street Journal* (September 8, 1994): 1+.

Chapter 12

1. Andrew E. Serwer, "How to Escape a Price War," *Fortune* 13 (June 1994): 84.

Chapter 13

1. Andrew Serwer, "How to Escape a Price War," *Fortune* (13 June 1994): 88.
2. W. David Gibson, "Going Off Patent: Keeping the Wolves from Your Door," *Sales & Marketing Management* (October 1990): 76–82.
3. Christopher Power, "Flops," *Business Week* (16 August 1993): 79.

Chapter 14

1. Brian Dumaine, "The Trouble with Teams," *Fortune* (September 5, 1994): 88.
2. Ibid., 88–90.
3. Tracy Carlson, "Brand Burnout," *Brandweek* (January 17, 1994): 26.
4. Zachary Schiller, Wendy Zellner, Ron Stodghill, and Mark Maremont, "Clout!" *Business Week* (December 21, 1992): 70.
5. Carlson, p. 27.
6. David Arnold, *The Handbook of Brand Management* (Reading, MA: Addison-Wesley, 1992): 226.
7. Ronald Henkoff, "Delivering the Goods," *Fortune* (November 28, 1994): 64.

Case Four

1. The information in this section is adapted with 3M permission from a workshop conducted by Bill Parfitt, June 7, 1991, and 3M promotional materials.
2. "Copy Chasers" column, *Business Marketing* (March 1989): 90-92.
3. James W. Obermayer, "Marrying Communications to Sales Dollars," *Business Marketing* (July 1998): 71.

GLOSSARY

Action program The part of the marketing plan describing the actual steps by which the marketing strategy is implemented to reach the established objectives.

Alpha test A method of testing a new product prototype within the developing company to eliminate potential defects before commercial launch. For example, a manufacturer of accounting software might test a new product within its own accounting department.

Benchmarking Comparing a product, a product feature, or a process against best-in-class to improve the level of quality.

Beta test A method of testing a new product prototype under actual customer-use situations to eliminate potential defects before commercial launch.

Brand equity The goodwill or positive identity of a brand.

Brand extension A slight variation of a product, carrying the brand name of the core product.

Brand manager The product manager title frequently used in consumer packaged goods.

Category killers Large-scale companies that have changed the way business is done in their industries by operating more cost effectively: for example, Wal-Mart in retailing, Home Depot in do-it-yourself home improvement, and W. W. Grainger in industrial distribution.

Causal forecasts Forecasts developed by studying the cause-and-effect relationships between variables: for example, housing starts might have a causal effect on the demand for private mortgage insurance.

Competitive intelligence The process of gathering, analyzing, and disseminating information on the competitive environment obtained through sales force input, on-line database searching, published sources, personal interviews, and so on.

Concept screening The evaluation of new-product ideas to determine whether they merit further analysis and development.

Concept testing The activity of taking new product ideas to customers for their input before further development.

Continuity Advertising on a continuous basis to the target market.

Contribution margin The amount of revenue left after incremental costs have been subtracted.

Contribution to overhead (CTO) The line on an income statement that indicates the amount of revenue left to cover overhead and profit after all direct and controllable costs have been subtracted.

Core competencies The central skills and knowledge of a company that provide its strengths against competition.

Customer visit program A method of qualitative marketing research whereby product managers visit customers as part of a team with the sole purpose of collecting market information (such as ideas for new products).

Delphi technique A method of reconciling subjective forecasts by using a sequential series of estimates derived from a panel of experts. Often used in forecasting technological change.

Distribution channel The set of all the firms and individuals that take title, or assist in transferring title, to a particular product or service as it moves from the producer to the customer.

Early indicator chart A chart of "red flags" that might indicate that a new-product launch is not moving at the pace required in the launch materials.

Fixed costs Costs that don't vary with production or sales level. Rent, heat, and executive salaries are examples of fixed costs.

Flanker brands Products created to reach a new market segment without altering the positioning of the main brand. For example, a new product or brand might be created for a low-priced segment of the market rather than reducing the price of the core product.

FMCG Fast-moving consumer goods.

Focus group A semistructured, free-flowing interview with a small group of customers, usually for the purpose of obtaining qualitative research.

Frame of reference The set of products a customer considers when making a purchase decision in a given product category.

Frequency The average number of times a customer sees an advertising message within a given time period.

Gross margin Sales revenue less cost of goods sold.

Incremental costs Costs that change with a decision to produce an additional quantity of product. These would include direct costs plus any semifixed costs (such as adding an additional shift) resulting from an increase in quantity produced.

Launch The introduction of new product to the market.

Launch control plan The identification of activities to be performed as part of new product commercialization, as well as the recognition of "red flags" to look for during the process.

Market segmentation The process of breaking a group of potential customers into smaller, more homogenous subsets.

Matrix organization An organizational structure in which individuals have both direct line (i.e., functional) reporting relationships as well as responsibilities to work horizontally with other groups in the company.

Milestone activities chart A list of the desired dates of completion for various "milestone" activities of a new-product launch, such as purchasing equipment, finalizing package design, and obtaining legal clearance.

New-product proposal A summary of a business plan for a new-product concept.

Parity Being perceived the same as all competitors, such as with commodity products.

Perceptual map A visual depiction of how customers position a product versus its competitors along identified factors.

Positioning statement A statement of how a product offering is to be perceived in the minds of customers relative to the competition.

Price sensitivity The degree to which a target market is motivated by price in making purchase decisions.

Product fact book A compilation of all information a company has on a product, its customers, and the product's competitors.

Product management team A cross-functional group used by some companies to make product management decisions in lieu of or in conjunction with product managers.

Prototype A mock-up or preliminary version of a new product used for research purposes.

Pulsing Grouping marketing communications within a given period of time to provide more intensity or impact than could be obtained from spreading those same communications evenly throughout the year.

Reach The number or percent of the target market being exposed to an advertising message within a given time period.

Regression A statistical method of relating a causal variable, such as an economic indicator, to sales. Future sales are then forecast by inserting the estimated causal variable into the equation.

Return on promotional investment (ROPI) A calculation of revenue generated directly from marketing communications, expressed as a percentage of the investment in those communications.

Roll-out The process of introducing a new product to the market by selectively prioritizing the markets and the order in which they receive the new product.

Segment management The process of organizing internal decisions and job roles by market segment rather than by product or function.

Share The portion of the overall sales in a market accounted for by a particular product, brand, or service. Also referred to as market share or share-of-market (SOM).

Standard Industrial Classification (SIC) Numeric government codes assigned to companies to designate the industry they are in.

Target market A market or portion of a market that a firm attempts to serve by actively allocating resources to it. Sometimes referred to as "served market."

Test marketing Taking a new product to a limited number of cities, companies, or geographic regions to test the effectiveness of a marketing strategy before the product is launched.

Unique selling proposition (USP) A term used to describe the primary competitive differentiation of a product or service to be addressed in marketing communications.

Variable costs Those costs that vary directly with the level of production. They tend to be constant per unit produced.

INDEX